FROM CRUMBS TO CONFIDENCE:

RISING ABOVE CHALLENGES IGNITING YOUR PURPOSE AND POWER

MARQUETTA TOSHE' HEMPHILL

I Got Donuts:
From Crumbs to Confidence

First Printing. Printed in the United States of America.

Published by A2Z Books Publishing Lithonia, GA 30058

www.A2ZBookspublishing.net

Manufactured in the United States of America.

Author has allowed this work to remain exactly as the author intended, verbatim.

This book is dedicated to the extraordinary people in my life who stood by me when the road got rough. While not everyone is named, please know that your unwavering support has been a cornerstone of my journey. Through every storm, you were the ones praying over me, lifting me up, and reminding me to keep my head held high—even on the days when I felt like giving up. Y'all's love and encouragement have been my anchor.

First and foremost, I gotta give all glory to God. Lord, you kept my head above water, spoke to me through dreams, and reminded me that You had the final say. Thank You for holding me down when I couldn't do it myself.

To my husband—you are the real MVP. Words could never fully express how much you mean to me. God made you specifically for me. All I can say is, if you know, you know! Period.

To my daughters—my "why," my light, my joy, my EVERYTHING. Y'all keep me grounded and make sure my heart stays full. Your laughter? Whew! That's the soundtrack to my soul. Y'all are my heartbeats, and I love you more than words can say.

To my mama—whew, that lady right there! I could write a whole separate book just about her. But for now, I'll keep it simple: I love her to pieces. Oh, and Da, you already know the inside joke: "Yep, you're fat!" (Don't worry, y'all, that's the family inside joke.)

To my brothers—listen, there's nobody like y'all. You are the best brothers a girl could ask for. Y'all always have my back, and I'm forever grateful. Love you more than warm chocolate chip cookies!

To "Da Bestie"—girl, you have been my rock. I admired your leadership style from day one—so genuine and so YOU. If it weren't for your guidance and encouragement, none of this would have been possible. #Lock&Key, you already know what's up!

To the "Cawfey Crew"—listen, I wouldn't have even had the courage to take this leap of faith without y'all. You both held me down, reminded me of my worth, and kept me laughing when I wanted to cry. And that book? You know it changed the game for me. Thank you for everything.

And last but certainly not least, my first intern, you are the G.O.A.T., no question. Your ambition and drive pushed me to be better, and this book wouldn't even exist without the impact you've had on my life. You are proof that mentorship is a two-way street.

To the countless friends and mentors who have poured into me, thank you for your guidance, prayers, and love. Y'all overflowed my cup, and I promise to keep pouring into others as you've poured into me.

Now, to the naysayers, the doubters, and the demotivators…I see you too! Thank you for the fuel. This book is part of my healing and my testimony. You gave me the push to find out who I truly am and step into my purpose. And guess what? Now I fully understand the saying: "Let your haters be your motivators!"

To everyone who played a role in my journey—good, bad, or indifferent, thank you. I love y'all to the core of my heart.

"This book is based on my personal experiences and perspectives. It does not intend to harm or defame any individual or organization."

CONTENTS

Introduction: The Purpose Behind the Pages   1

Not Everyone Who Looks Like "YOU" is for "YOU"!   3

The Illusion of "I Got Donuts" Leadership   5

Standing Strong and Overcoming Obstacles   7

Blooming Where Planted: From Legacy to Lessons   10

Faith as the Foundation   13

Walking Away with Wisdom   16

Georgia: A Fresh Start   19

A New Beginning   21

Breaking Into Corporate America   26

The Donut Paradox: Redefining Leadership Through Resilience   36

The Donut Trap: When Seeking Support Becomes a Challenge   38

Donuts and Dynamics: Navigating Leadership Challenges   40

The Final Straw (a.k.a. The Moment I Knew I Was Done)   42

Drowning in Donuts: Finding Myself in Chaos   44

From Donuts to Destiny: A Dream, A Song, and a Breakthrough   47

Breaking the Glaze: Leadership and Growth Reflections   54

From Donuts to Destiny: A Shift in the Making   56

The Lesson I Learned   60

Pouring Into Others   62

Standing in My Truth   63

What's With Donuts?   64

Navigating Through the Assortment of Donuts   67

Exercise One: Recognizing the Donuts for What They Are   71

Exercise Two: Learning From the Donuts and Identify the Gap   75

Exercise Three: Experiencing Your Shift   78

Exercise Four: Building Your Roadmap   81

Exercise Five: Pouring Into Others   85

Exercise Six: Staying Motivated   87

Exercise Seven: Embrace the Bigger Picture   90

Exercise Eight: Find Motivation in Mentorship   92

Exercise Nine: Choose Joy Daily   94

Exercise Ten: Moving Forward   96

Closing Thoughts: Don't Let the Donuts Roll!   98

INTRODUCTION:
THE PURPOSE BEHIND THE PAGES

They say that in every workplace, you'll meet people who challenge, inspire, and sometimes even betray you. For me, the workplace has been a battlefield –a place where dreams meet reality, ambition is tested, and growth often comes at the cost of hard lessons learned. My journey has been one of resilience, self-discovery, and, above all, authenticity. I am writing this book to share my story: a story about building a brand that stands firm in the face of adversity, about navigating the challenges of corporate life as a minority woman, and about overcoming obstacles thrown at you by people you thought had your back.

A personal brand is more than a buzzword; it is your identity, reputation, and values, all wrapped into one. It is how you show up, how you are remembered, and what you stand for. For years, I did not fully understand the power of a personal brand. I thought hard work and dedication would be enough to climb the corporate ladder. I believed that if I delivered results, my path to success would unfold naturally.

The workplace has taught me a lot. In this world, your brand is not just a nice-to-have; it is your trademark, shield, and greatest survival tool. It is what protects you when opportunities pass you by, when your hard work goes unnoticed, or when people try to diminish your worth or discredit your contributions. It is what ensures that, even when others attempt to write your narrative, your truth, and integrity stand firm, speaking louder than any detractors ever could.

Your brand is what sets you apart in rooms where you may feel invisible, and it gives you the strength to persevere when the challenges feel threatening. It is not about crafting a perfect image or creating a façade; it is about knowing who you are at your core and letting that truth shine through in everything you do. It is about being consistent in your values, your actions, and your intentions, regardless of the circumstances around you.

Building a personal brand is an act of self-discovery and empowerment. It is about embracing your authenticity and understanding that your unique qualities—whether it is your perspective, your experiences, or your voice—are your greatest assets. It is about standing firm in your identity, even when the odds are stacked against you, and refusing to let anyone force you into a box that does not align with your truth. The workforce taught me that having a strong brand is not just an advantage—it is a necessity. It is the foundation upon which you build your resilience, your confidence, and your ability to rise above.

NOT EVERYONE WHO LOOKS LIKE "YOU" IS FOR "YOU"!

Adversity is something I have faced more times than I can count. From the moment I entered the workforce, I realized that this space came with unique challenges. Microaggressions, biases, and systemic barriers were part of the terrain. But what hurt the most were the obstacles placed in my path by people I thought I could trust—people who looked like me and who I believed would support me.

During my journey, I experienced leaders who I initially believed would be my ally. The sight of their position filled me with hope, and they represented what I aspired to achieve. I thought to myself, finally, someone who understands what it is like to navigate these spaces not just as a woman, but as a minority in the workplace. I envisioned leaders as guides, mentors, and individuals who could help me decode the complexities of my career and show me the ropes.

But what I hoped for and what I received were two entirely different realities. Instead of support, I was met with resistance. Instead of mentorship, I faced manipulation. Instead of collaboration, there was competition. I have encountered leaders who used their positions not to uplift but to make the journey harder.

Here was someone who I thought would understand the unique struggles of being a woman in the workplace, and I believed who would see me as someone to influence and support, just as I hoped to do for others one day. Instead, I felt I was a threat. Their actions were not just a personal attack; they were a reminder that not everyone who looks like you is for you.

This realization hit me hard. It is one thing to face obstacles from people who do not share your experiences, who may not understand your perspective. But to face that kind of betrayal from someone who shares your identity is a different level of pain. It challenged everything I thought I knew about solidarity and support among women in the workplace.

Despite these obstacles, I learned some of the most valuable lessons along the way. My experiences have taught me that leadership is not defined by position or power but by how you use it. It is about pouring into others, not tearing them down. It is about creating opportunities, not hoarding them. It is about collaboration, not competition.

My experiences also forced me to look inward. I had to ask myself; *how will I lead when I am in a leadership position? What kind of example will I set?* I promised myself then and there that I would never lead with fear, insecurity, or scarcity. I would lead with confidence, generosity, and abundance. I would be the mentor who guides, uplifts, and empowers others.

THE ILLUSION OF "I GOT DONUTS" LEADERSHIP

One of the most vivid metaphors from my career path is what I call the "I Got Donuts" leadership style. Picture this: a leader walks into the office with a box of donuts, smiling from ear to ear, as if this simple gesture can magically erase the real issues plaguing the team. To the unsuspecting eye, it might seem thoughtful—a sweet treat to boost morale. But to those paying attention, it becomes clear that this is nothing more than a band-aid fix, a quick attempt to mask the lack of real leadership, strategy, and care.

Donuts are easy. They are sweet, temporary, and ultimately hollow. They do not address the deeper issues within a team. They do not foster trust, improve processes, or develop talent. They certainly do not provide the foundation for true growth or long-term success. The "I Got Donuts" leadership approach is a classic example of performative gestures—actions that give the appearance of care and engagement but lack any real substance.

Leadership is not about superficial gestures. While donuts and pizza parties are fun in the moment, they do not sustain a team through challenges or inspire people to excel. Leadership is about showing up for your team in ways that matter. It is about investing in people, nurturing their talents, and empowering them to succeed. It is about creating an environment where individuals feel valued, heard, and supported. Meanwhile, "I Got Donuts" leadership, on the other hand, ignores all of that. Instead, it opts for quick, shallow wins that require neither accountability nor true commitment.

Let us be clear: leadership is not about the donuts; it is about the delivery. And I do not mean the delivery of sweet treats —I mean the delivery of genuine support, actionable guidance, and meaningful connections. What people remember is not the glazed donuts you brought to the office but the ways you helped them grow, the times you stood in their corner, and the moments you empowered them to achieve their potential.

The problem with "I Got Donuts" leadership is that it is a cop-out. It is a way to appear engaged without doing the actual work of leading. True leadership requires intentionality, accountability, and a willingness to roll up your sleeves and do the hard work of developing people. It requires creating a culture of trust and collaboration, where individuals know their contributions are valued and their growth is prioritized.

Do not get me wrong; there is nothing wrong with bringing donuts or hosting a fun team event. Those things are great for team bonding and morale. But they should never be used as a substitute for real leadership. They are the sprinkles on top, not the substance.

The takeaway? Leadership is not about showing up with a box of donuts —it is about showing up for your team in ways that matter. It is about being present, intentional, and committed to creating an environment where everyone can thrive. Leadership is not about quick fixes or hollow gestures; it is about laying a solid foundation that empowers others to reach their fullest potential. And no donut, no matter how sweet, can ever replace that.

STANDING STRONG AND OVERCOMING OBSTACLES

Despite these challenges, I refused to let adversity define me. Every obstacle became an opportunity to learn, grow, and strengthen my resolve. I realized that while I could not control the actions of others, I could control how I responded. I had a choice: allow betrayal and disappointment to consume me, or use them as fuel to propel me forward.

I chose the latter. I began to focus on what I could control: my work ethic, my integrity, and personal brand. I stopped looking for validation from others and started validating myself.

I learned to advocate for myself, speak up even when it was uncomfortable, and demand the respect I deserved. I also learned to set boundaries, recognize toxic relationships, and walk away from situations that did not serve me.

One of the most powerful lessons I have learned is that resilience does not mean being unaffected by hardship. It means feeling the pain, processing it, and coming out stronger on the other side. It means refusing to let adversity steal your joy or dim your light. It means showing up as your authentic self, no matter how uncomfortable that makes others.

As a mentor and leader, I carry that lesson with me every day. I know what it feels like to be unsupported, doubted, and have someone actively work against you. And because **I HAVE BEEN THERE**, I am intentional about creating spaces where others feel valued, heard, and empowered.

Final Thoughts

I am writing this book because I know my story is not unique. It reflects the journeys of countless individuals who navigate professional spaces, striving to be seen, heard, and valued. Many of us have faced moments that tested our resilience, made us question our worth, and challenged our path forward. This book is for those who have felt overlooked, underestimated, and undervalued. It is for those who have struggled with workplace dynamics, encountered difficult leadership, or wrestled with self-doubt along the way.

But more importantly, I am writing this book to offer hope. I want to show that it is possible to overcome adversity, reclaim your power, and build a personal brand that reflects your true self. I want to inspire others to rise above obstacles, stay true to their values, and lead with authenticity and purpose.

This book is a testament to resilience, self-discovery, and the power of investing in people rather than relying on surface-level solutions. Leadership is not about quick fixes or empty gestures — it is about showing up, doing the work, and creating real opportunities for growth. It is about fostering an environment where people feel valued, heard, and empowered to succeed.

As you read this book, I hope you will see reflections of your own journey within my story. I hope you will be inspired to assess your own brand, set your own standards, and define the legacy you want to leave behind. Building a personal brand is not about perfection; it is about being intentional, authentic, and unapologetically yourself. It is about standing firm in your values, even when the world tries to shake you.

It is about rising above challenges— not just for yourself, but for those who will come after you.

This is my story. This is my journey. And this is my truth.

Welcome to "I Got Donuts!"

BLOOMING WHERE PLANTED: FROM LEGACY TO LESSONS

Growing up, my grandparents were the heartbeat of my life. They were not just caregivers; they were the blueprint for how I wanted to show up in the world. They were walking brands before I ever knew what branding meant— recognized not just for what they did, but for who they were. Their actions, work, presence, and everything about them left an indelible impression.

My granddaddy, Mr. "Nailbender," embodied hard work and craftsmanship. He could take an ordinary piece of wood and transform it into something extraordinary. When he put on his blue-and-white pinstriped overalls, slid his hammer into the belt loop, and grabbed his receipt book, it was like watching a superhero suit up. He didn't just build things — he built trust, reputation, and legacy.

I will never forget riding in the back of his orange and white 1970 Chevy C-10 pickup truck. That was freedom. That was joy. Wind in my face, laughter in my heart, and the feeling that this was what security looked like —being part of something strong, something real. Whether we were pulling weeds in the garden, hauling lumber, or simply watching him bring a piece of wood to life, I learned an invaluable truth: greatness does not just happen— it is cultivated.

Then there was my grandmama — "Big Momma." Stylish does not even begin to describe her. She did not just wear clothes; she wore confidence. Shopping with her was an event. Hats, suits, shoes—you name it, she had them coordinated down to the earrings. Big Momma didn't just step out; she stepped up—every day, as her best self. Watching her walk the runway at local fashion shows was mesmerizing. She did not just model clothes; she modeled pride, self-respect, and the art of commanding attention without saying a word.

Together, my grandparents were "The Walkers"—and that name meant something in the community. Their home reflected the same excellence and pride they carried in their everyday lives. The lawn? Flawless. The flowers? Arranged like artwork. And inside? The air was thick with the scent of Southern cooking and love. Whether it was the hum of a pot of greens on the stove or the sweet aroma of a fresh pound cake cooling on the counter, their home was an experience, not just a place.

Hospitality was not just what they did; it was who they were. When you walked through their door, you were welcomed with a smile that radiated love, a flash of their pearly whites (and that one twinkling gold tooth!), and an immediate offer of sweet tea, a Coke, or ice water. They made you feel valued without even trying.

Reflecting on their legacy now, I see that they were teaching me about branding long before I had the words to describe it. Branding is not just about logos, labels, or marketing, it is about identity. It is about what you stand for, how you make people feel, and the impression you leave behind. My grandparents did not need business cards or flashy titles, their actions, integrity, and unwavering pride spoke for them.

I did not realize it at the time, but every lesson they taught me was shaping my own brand. Your name, your reputation—is your brand. When people hear your name, what comes to mind? Are you dependable? Are you respected? Are you someone who leaves people better than you found them? These are the questions I have carried with me as I have navigated my own journey.

Everything I have become is a reflection of what they instilled in me. The lessons they lived—not just taught—became the foundation for how I lead, how I work, and how I show up in the world.

FAITH AS THE FOUNDATION

While my grandparents taught me about setting high standards and living with pride, my mother gave me the spiritual grounding I would need to weather life's storms. Faith was not just something we practiced —it was our foundation. Church was more than a Sunday routine; it was a lifestyle, a classroom, and a support system all in one. It was where I learned resilience, community, and the power of service.

And let me tell you, when Sunday came around, we showed up. My mama believed in honoring God not just in prayer but in presentation. And baby, when I say church was an event, I mean it. It was not just a place of worship —it was where people came together, where we celebrated, supported, and uplifted one another. The congregation was not just a room full of churchgoers— it was family.

For a young girl with big dreams and even bigger personality, church was a place of value, a space where you could show up as your authentic self, feel a sense of belonging, and be accepted.

One of the most defining experiences of my church life was being part of the youth ministry. And as one of the "OG youth members," I took pride in setting an example. We were the first class to participate in the church's Youth Pageant — a prestigious, highly anticipated event that showcased our journey in faith and personal growth.

But this was not just any pageant. This was a competition. And if you know me, you already know I do not do anything halfway. If there is a title to win, best believe I am bringing my A-game.

This pageant was no exception. We were judged on everything —
journaling, scrapbooking, and public speaking. I was ready. I scrap-
booked like I was crafting a visual Picasso. I commanded the stage
during public speaking like I had been doing it my whole life. By the
time the final scores were being tallied, I was already wearing that
crown in my mind.

Then, the night of the pageant arrived.

We stood on stage in our pure white debutante gowns, glowing under
the church lights. My heart was racing as the hostess began announc-
ing the winners.

Second-place runner-up was called. It was not me. My confidence
soared.

Then came the first-place runner-up.

And my name rang out: "Marquetta Toshe' Price."

Wait. What?

I was first-place runner-up, not the winner.

Confusion hit me like a ton of bricks. I had won four out of five cate-
gories. So, what happened? After the event, the program director
pulled my mother aside. In a hushed tone, she said:

"It came down to one point."

One. Point.

But then came the real blow.

"Marquetta was a wonderful participant, but little girls are to be seen and not heard. She is too loud, too outgoing, and not girly enough. She needs molding."

Molding!?

At that moment, I realized that I was not being judged on my talent or my dedication — I was being judged on my personality.

That was devastating. I thought, "Since when was being Marquetta a problem?"

I did not choose this personality. It was God-given.

Yet, here I was, being told that who I was needed "fixing." That my confidence was too bold, too loud, too much. That my authenticity was not enough.

WALKING AWAY WITH WISDOM

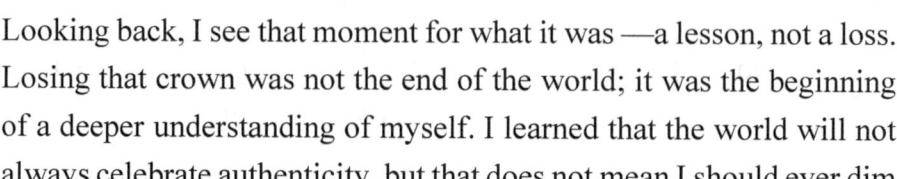

Looking back, I see that moment for what it was —a lesson, not a loss. Losing that crown was not the end of the world; it was the beginning of a deeper understanding of myself. I learned that the world will not always celebrate authenticity, but that does not mean I should ever dim my light.

My grandparents taught me legacy, my mother rooted me in faith, and this experience…Well, it solidified my strength. The crown was not mine, but the wisdom I gained that night was something no one could ever take away.

So, when I stepped into my first retail job in college, I walked in with lessons in my back pocket and ambition in my heart. Y'all, I loved that job! It was more than just a paycheck — it was my first taste of independence, a chance to grow, lead, and, of course, serve looks while doing it. Because let's be clear, being "Marquetta Chic and stunning on 'em" was always part of the package.

I was the youngest employee on the team, which only made me hungrier to prove myself. While some people clocked in and out without a second thought, I was soaking up knowledge like a biscuit in gravy. I learned how the store operated, how sales worked, even how to handle finances. My drive was undeniable.

Then came the opportunity. A lead position opened, and I knew this was my moment. I had been preparing without even realizing it, learning store operations, tracking metrics, and getting my finances together. So, I boldly put my name in the hat.

When my senior leader called me in, I just knew I had it.

She started with praise:

"Marquetta, you're doing an amazing job. Your ambition and energy are unmatched. You're always willing to learn, and it shows."

My chest puffed up. Yes! She sees it. She gets it.

Then came the infamous "but."

"But you're just too young. You're not ready yet."

Whew. There it was.

The words hung in the air like a stale donut. My stomach dropped. Not ready? What does my age have to do with my ability? I had heard this song before, just with different lyrics. "Too young." "Too bold." "Too much." That moment lit a fire in me—not one that burned me down, but one that fueled me forward.

It was becoming painfully clear that this was not just about age. It was about perception. About how people see you through the narrow lens of their own biases. About how they place limits on you because they cannot —or choose not to— see the fullness of your potential.

At that moment, everything clicked. Every time I had been told I needed to "adjust," "conform," or "tone it down" flashed before me.

But that was the shift:

I realized it was never about me. Their words, their biases, their inability to see my value? That was their issue, not mine. I refused to let their narrow vision define my future. I would use their doubt as fuel, their biases as motivation, and their barriers as stepping stones.

Their inability to see my worth? That was not my burden to carry. From that moment on, I knew that every "no" was not a rejection, it was a redirection.

I did not stay at that job much longer. I realized I was not going to be handed a seat at the table — or maybe I was just at the wrong table altogether.

So, I packed up my ambition, my lessons, and of course, my fabulous wardrobe, and walked away. Not out of defeat, but out of clarity.

And guess what? It happened again.

At another job, another leadership opportunity arose. I applied, confident that this time would be different. But guess what?

"You are not ready yet."

Y'all. At this point, that phrase was becoming a recurring character in the sitcom of my life. It popped up at the worst times, always stealing the spotlight. And slowly, it started affecting me. I started hiding parts of myself. I toned down my personality, my ideas, my shine. I figured if I fit into their mold, maybe, just maybe, I would finally be seen as "ready."

But let me tell you something. That was not me. I had dreams. A vision so clear, it lived rent-free in my head. I wanted to lead. To bring fresh ideas. To make an impact. And yet, it felt like being myself was the very thing standing in the way.

That was the moment I asked myself: "Why does being Marquetta feel like a setback when I am working so hard for a come-up?"

GEORGIA:
A FRESH START

In 2012, my husband came to me with an opportunity that could change everything for our family. His job was relocating to Georgia, and he wanted us to move with him. Without hesitation, the girls and I said YES. Georgia was calling, and it felt like the fresh start we all needed.

Excitement ran through my veins as we packed up our lives. This was more than just a move—this was a reset. A chance to realign, reinvent, and step into something new. I did not know a soul in Georgia, and no one knew me. That was the beauty of it. I had a blank canvas to build the brand I wanted—the one that would take me into boardrooms, leadership positions, and decision-making spaces. Georgia was bursting with possibility, and I was ready to seize it.

While I was laying the foundation for my next move, my husband was thriving in his corporate career, climbing the ladder with ease. Watching him succeed filled me with so much pride, but it also lit a fire in me.

We started attending corporate events—work parties, luncheons, networking mixers. If you have ever seen those glossy TV shows with the picture-perfect corporate world, this was it.

Let me set the scene:

Husbands clinked glasses, sipping top-shelf liquor, while we wives stood in little circles, engaging in small talk that was anything but small.

But here was the twist—these women were not just "corporate wives." They were powerhouses. Senior leaders. Women holding the very titles I dreamed of.

They talked about boardroom battles, strategic wins, and high-stakes decisions like it was just another day at the office. And then there was me—working in retail, standing there feeling like I did not belong. Let me be clear: Nobody made me feel that way.

It was me.

Every time someone asked where I worked or what I did, I cringed. As if retail was not enough. As if I was not enough.

And then came the real gut punch:

I started doubting my own name. Was "Marquetta" too much? Too ghetto? Did my name belong in these spaces? I was forming unconscious biases against myself that I did not even know existed.

The shame was not coming from them—it was coming from ME. These women? They were kind, supportive, and genuinely interested in my story. They were **not looking down on me** I was looking down on myself.

I was damn good at my job. But at that moment, I just could not see it.

A New Beginning

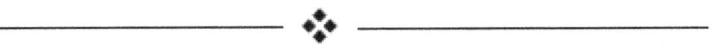

With our move to Georgia, I was determined to prove myself. This was my chance to shine—a fresh start, where no one knew me, and my work would speak for itself. With my background in retail, I climbed the ranks quickly and became an Assistant Store Manager. Y'all, I was on fire. This was not just a promotion—it was a platform.

Then, the perfect opportunity landed in my lap. The Store Manager went on maternity leave. This was my moment. My chance to step up, prove I was ready, and show them I was more than capable.

And let me tell you, I DELIVERED.

I turned the store around, boosted morale, improved sales, and led my team like I had been running things forever. Week after week, I poured my energy, strategy, and passion into making sure the store thrived. Then came the news that felt like divine alignment: the Store Manager decided not to return.

Y'all, I cannot even describe the level of excitement and anticipation I felt. This was it. The position was mine. I had been doing the job already. I had proven my value, outworked expectations, and led my team like a seasoned Store Manager. I could feel it in my bones—this was the moment I had been working for.

When the District Manager called me, I was ready. The conversation was flowing effortlessly, and her excitement made me even more confident.

And then…

She said it…

"Marquetta, I see your passion, but… you are not ready."

Y'ALL!!!!

It felt like the air had been sucked out of the room. I sat there, stunned. My mind was racing.

Not ready?!

NOT READY?!

What else could I have done? I turned the store around! I led the team. I did everything right.

How was I not ready?

I nodded, forcing myself to look professional, but inside, I was spiraling.

Was there a hidden checklist I missed?

Was there a secret manual about my life that no one gave me?

Was I just not in on the joke?!

It felt like no matter how hard I worked, how much I proved myself, or how many wins I secured, I was always being told "not yet."

And let me tell y'all—I kept it cool on the outside, but on the inside, I was screaming.

And then… she walked in.

With a big, overly enthusiastic grin, she plopped a box of donuts on the counter and cheerfully announced:

"I GOT DONUTS!"

Y'all!

I. SAW. RED!

After everything that had just happened, she thought DONUTS were the solution?! As if pastries could somehow erase the fact that I had just been dismissed, overlooked, and ignored? As if glaze and sprinkles were supposed to fill the void of actual leadership?

Donuts?! Really?!

If I could have thrown that box across the store, I would have. But instead, I mustered up every ounce of sarcasm in my being, looked her dead in the eye, and said:

"No thanks, I already had breakfast."

Y'all, I was DONE.

What I wanted was guidance. What I needed was for her to sit down with me and say:

"Marquetta, here's what I see. Here's where you are excelling. Here's where you can grow. Let's build a plan to get you where you want to go."

I needed her to acknowledge my hard work.

To mentor me.

To invest in me.

But instead of offering me growth, she offered me donuts. And THAT was the moment everything changed.

Because here is what I realized:

- Leadership is not about walking in with a box of donuts.

- Leadership is about showing up with REAL guidance, REAL support, and REAL mentorship.

- Leadership is about investing in people, not pacifying them with empty gestures.

And the biggest slap in the face?

They brought in a new Store Manager—someone completely unfit for the job. Morale tanked. Customers left. Employees quit. The store fell apart.

And then, guess who came crawling back? The District Manager.

Suddenly, they wanted me…

Suddenly, they saw my value…

Suddenly, they were practically begging me to take the job.

But by then?

I was DONE. I learned my lesson.

I knew my worth, and it was no longer tied to a job that refused to recognize it.

The Turning Point

That experience changed me. I realized I did not need to stay in spaces that did not value me. I did not need to keep proving myself to people who refused to see my worth. So, I did what any self-respecting, growth-focused woman would do—I put in my notice and LEFT.

And guess what?

That store eventually closed.

My decision to walk away was not just the right one—it was ON TIME.

That moment solidified a promise to myself:

- I would never let anyone else's opinion define my potential.

- I was done waiting for permission to be great.

- I was done dimming my light to fit into a mold that was never made for me.

And most importantly?

I was done accepting donuts as a substitute for real leadership. That moment of clarity lit a fire in me, and I knew it was time to make a major move. Later that evening, I sat down with my husband, venting about how I was over retail.

"I want something new. I want what you have. I want to work in corporate."

I had always admired the stability, the structure, and the impact of corporate roles. It was about more than just a paycheck. It was about building something. Growing. Thriving.

BREAKING INTO CORPORATE AMERICA

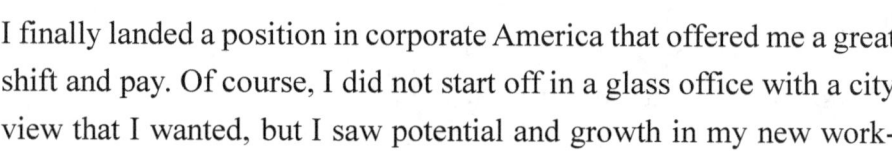

I finally landed a position in corporate America that offered me a great shift and pay. Of course, I did not start off in a glass office with a city view that I wanted, but I saw potential and growth in my new workplace. I wasn't doing my dream job, but I felt closer than ever to achieving it.

I had never worked in this field before, but I enjoyed learning something completely new and adding a new skill to my resume. I was overjoyed because I was surrounded by women who held senior leadership positions. They became my role models and people who I aspired to become. They were so down-to-earth yet highly respected throughout the workplace.

These women made decisions of power and when they spoke, their presence alone commanded attention. Though I was new to the company, these women had already established and made an awesome brand for themselves. With their knowledge and expertise, they were assets to any business in our industry.

While in that role, I was determined to make the most of every opportunity. So I embraced every chance to learn. If there was a door even slightly cracked open, I was going to nudge my way through. I was on a mission to make a name for myself and to soak up every ounce of knowledge I could about the business. Beyond the day-to-day grind, I threw myself into every program and event I could find. One of those opportunities led me to a mentor—a mentor who would become a pivotal figure in my career and life.

This mentor wasn't just anyone; he was a master connector and teacher. He guided and propelled me. I looked forward to our monthly meetings, where he advised and exposed me to people and opportunities. He introduced me to a network of professionals who didn't just talk about success; they lived it. He helped me see beyond my current role, and map out how I could climb the corporate ladder. And y'all, when I tell you this mentorship was transformative, I mean it. It wasn't just about the advice—it was about having someone in my corner who truly believed in me.

As I grew in that role, so did my confidence. I fell in love with this new version of Marquetta—bold, knowledgeable, and ready to take on the world. I started sharing my newfound wisdom with my coworkers, encouraging them to see beyond the four walls we worked in daily. I wanted them to see what I saw: opportunities to grow, to learn, and to build something greater for themselves. If there was a benefit or resource out there, I made sure they knew about it. That's just who I am. If I eat, we all eat.

Now, let me set the scene for y'all: working in that environment wasn't always glamorous. If it was cold outside, it was cold inside. If it was hot, we would sweat like we were in a sauna. And don't even get me started on the uninvited "guests". You know, the non-human ones with more legs than you'd like to see. But despite all that, I made sure we had fun. Because if we were going to work hard, we might as well enjoy ourselves. And y'all know I'm always going to bring the energy!

But here's the part that really got under my skin: the reward system. **Donuts**. Yep, you read that right. **Donuts**. After all our hard work, the leadership team thought the best way to show appreciation for our efforts was to bring in a box of glazed pastries. Now, I love a good donut as much as the next person, but seriously? This was how they chose to show appreciation? Not by teaching us new skills or creating opportunities, but by handing us sugar-coated carbs. Y'all, I was fed up— glazed over fed up.

Instead of investing in people, leadership kept falling back on these superficial gestures. And it wasn't just me who felt this way. I could see the frustration in my coworkers' faces. We deserved better. My mentor had shown me what real leadership looked like—supporting people in their career journeys, guiding them, and opening doors for them. That's the kind of leader I wanted to be. Someone who handed out opportunities and not donuts. The more I thought about it, the clearer it became that I needed something better. Something bigger. Something meaningful.

As I reflected on my next steps, I noticed a shift in our leadership team and the culture we had worked so hard to build. The executive women I admired—who inspired me with their vision and resilience—started leaving, one by one. With their departures, the heartbeat of our workplace seemed to fade. Processes unraveled, morale plummeted, and the sense of unity we once cherished disappeared. And then, as if the instability was not enough, the hammer dropped: a reorganization was taking place in our department. Everything was shifting, and I knew this would be a turning point.

After three years in that role, we were blindsided with the news that we had to reapply for our jobs. The uncertainty was overwhelming, and tensions were high. My husband, ever the supportive partner, immediately began making calls and reaching out to his network to see what could be done to secure my position. Meanwhile, I found myself navigating this whirlwind of change, leaning heavily on my faith and the invaluable lessons my mentor had instilled in me.

Then came the moment that left me stunned when a Human Resources manager approached me with a smirk. They leaned in and said, "Oh, just because you know people, you thought you had the upper hand?"

And then laughed.

Y'ALL.

I was floored. I never said that. I never even thought that. But that moment told me everything I needed to know.

And sure enough, when the selections were announced, the loud, outspoken Marquetta did not make the cut. But rather than despair, I put my full trust in God. I knew He had a plan, and that this closed door was leading me toward something greater. I felt an unexpected peace about it all, knowing my path was already being laid out.

Thanks to my mentor's unwavering support and guidance, I was able to land a new opportunity within the company. I was only out of work for a month—BUT GOD! The timing was divine, and I was eager to hit the ground running. Once again, y'all, I was ready to make my mark. After nailing the interview and officially getting hired, I was excited. You know that feeling when you think, this is it! This is another fresh start and opportunity. I was all in, ready to bring my energy and ambition to this new chapter.

But then reality set in. You know that moment when you realize the job you interviewed for and the job that you are actually doing are two completely different things? Yeah, that was the role. It quickly became apparent that this was not the ideal position I had envisioned. To make things more complicated, I found myself back in retail—the very environment I had worked so hard to leave behind. And let me tell you, this time, it came with a whole new set of challenges. I encountered every kind of attitude and personality you could imagine, from overly demanding customers to coworkers with their own quirks and agendas. It was a constant juggling act, and it tested every ounce of patience I had.

I felt deflated, like I had taken a step backward instead of forward. This line of work didn't feel like a good fit, and it certainly didn't feel like a place where I could grow. I started beating myself up...AGAIN. *Why am I here? What am I supposed to be learning?* It was one of those moments where doubt creeps in and tries to steal your joy. But deep down, I reminded myself that every experience—no matter how frustrating or uncomfortable—was shaping me. There was a lesson here, even if I couldn't see it yet.

You are probably reading this and thinking, *"Dang girl, what is wrong with you? Do you even know what you want? Do you know what makes you happy?"* And to answer that honestly—no, I couldn't have told you what I truly wanted. It was hard to put into words, but I knew one thing for certain: this wasn't it. The feeling I had, the dissatisfaction gnawing at me, was undeniable. Still, I looked forward to my monthly meetings with my mentor. Those moments kept me grounded and reminded me of the bigger picture. I did not complain about my role because I was genuinely grateful for the opportunity, but inside, I was deeply unhappy. I felt stuck, lost, and unsure of how to find my way out of the fog.

One day, during a particularly emotional venting session with my mom, she stopped me mid-rant and hit me with a quote that changed everything. She said, *"You know what Maya Angelou says? 'If you don't like something, change it. If you can't change it, change your attitude.'"* Y'all, those words landed like a lightning bolt. Something in me shifted immediately. That simple, powerful truth ignited a spark of determination and motivation that I had not felt in a long time.

From that moment, I decided to approach my role differently. The negativity surrounding the job and the comments about its limitations no longer fazed me. Instead of focusing on what I didn't like, I channeled my energy into finding ways to elevate the position. I began identifying opportunities to improve processes, streamline operations, and create more value in the role.

This mindset shift unlocked a new sense of purpose, and it didn't go unnoticed. Not only did I experience personal satisfaction but I also connected with new mentors who saw my potential. That one conversation with my mom, and that quote, became a turning point, a reminder that even when the situation seems out of control, your attitude and perspective can make all the difference.

This progress propelled me into a role I absolutely loved. My director was phenomenal, recognizing the potential in me that I hadn't yet seen in myself. This position was a blank canvas, allowing me to connect with people from diverse backgrounds, motivate and influence others, and fulfill my passion for "pouring into others." It became my platform for honoring my mentors' guidance by giving back and supporting others in their journeys.

Even though I absolutely LOVED this role, my ultimate goal was to earn a "manager" title. While I was deeply fulfilled by influencing people and helping them grow, I wanted to take my impact further by shaping the business itself. I envisioned myself contributing at a higher level, driving strategy, and making decisions that would influence not just individuals but entire teams and processes. The next step on the career ladder—becoming a manager felt like the natural progression.

One of the most pivotal opportunities I had in pursuit of this goal was participating in an employee internship opportunity. This experience was transformative. It allowed me to step outside of my daily responsibilities and immerse myself in a completely different department within the company. Through this program, I connected with incredible professionals who shared their expertise and provided me with invaluable insights.

The projects I worked on during this internship were not just about completing tasks, they were about seeing the bigger picture. I gained a high-level understanding of how the company operated, how decisions were made, and how various departments intertwined to drive business success. This bird's eye view was eye-opening, giving me the knowledge and confidence to speak intelligently about broader organizational strategies. It also helped me see where my skills and passions could make the most significant impact.

By taking on stretch projects that challenged me to think beyond my current role, I developed a deeper understanding of business operations and learned how to communicate effectively with leadership. These experiences became key talking points as I continued to shape my career path. They provided me with the tools and insights I needed to position myself as someone ready to take on greater responsibilities. This Gig assignment wasn't just a project, it was a launchpad for my career aspirations. It gave me the clarity, confidence, and connections I needed to prepare for the next chapter of my professional journey.

I truly enjoyed interning with the team. For the first time, I truly saw how business decisions were made. I was so excited to see projects come down the pipeline and get assigned. I was the front face of the business! If you could have seen the passion and excitement in my eyes, you would have thought I was a kid in a candy store. This opportunity helped me develop the skills necessary for my next promotion: becoming a manager.

One afternoon, I was looking through the list of open job roles and came across one that sparked my interest. It was in a field I had always told my mentor I was passionate about. One nugget that I was taught when coming into the corporate sector was, *"Why not apply, the worst thing they can say* is no". So, after discussing it with my husband, we agreed—I should go for it. Even though I didn't have direct experience in the field, I took a risk and applied.

About a week later, I had my first interview with the recruiter which was pretty much a screening. I spoke about all my past roles and the impact that I had made while in those roles. The conversation went well, but I didn't think too much about it. In my experience, job interviews were a rollercoaster and I would never get excited by them because of my history of being let down. I hate going into interviews, giving it my best, knowing I'm qualified, only to get that dreadful email stating the infamous line, *"We have decided not to move forward with your application"*. Y'all, that feeling HURTS LIKE HELL!!! Especially when you know you are more than qualified for the role, position, job, or whatever you want to call it.

The following week I received a meeting invitation for a second-round interview. I was amazed! This time the interview was with the hiring manager. In my mind from past hurt, I was skeptical, but I talked myself into it and remained positive. We had a great interview, and I felt this leader was relatable. I thought to myself, *finally*, I get to work alongside a leader who I felt could truly understand my journey and support my growth. This got me even more excited and eager for the opportunity. This time, I would have a "role model" in senior leadership who could understand my struggle, and support me in getting to the next level.

Long story short, after three rounds of interviews and an impatient Marquetta (nearly pulling the strands out of my favorite wig), the OFFER LETTER finally hit my inbox! I got the job! Y'all, I had tears of joy. This was the opportunity I had been waiting for. At that moment, it felt like everything was aligning perfectly.

I wasted no time sharing the news with my family, friends, and mentors. They had been cheering me on from the sidelines, and this win felt like something we could all celebrate. It felt like a dream come true, the start of something big, something meaningful. I was ready to hit the ground running, to learn, to grow, and to make my mark. This was it, the beginning of my career glow-up! This is what I had been wanting for myself to prove that I am capable!

This role was exactly what I envisioned—a blank canvas where I could bring fresh ideas and make a real impact just as I had done in my previous positions. However, this was an entirely new area of business for me, and I had a lot to learn. I approached it the way I approach any new role: as a sponge, ready to absorb everything I needed to know to succeed.

My process has always been clear and consistent—learn the business, identify opportunities for improvement, and then execute. This simple yet effective blueprint has been the foundation of my success in every role I have held. And with this new opportunity, I was ready to put it into action once again.

THE DONUT PARADOX:
REDEFINING LEADERSHIP
THROUGH RESILIENCE

When I stepped into my new position, I was filled with excitement and ambition. This was the opportunity I had been waiting for—a chance to make a significant impact, showcase my skills, and grow as a leader. I came in with confidence and a vision for what I wanted to achieve. I knew that learning the ropes would take time, but I was determined to roll up my sleeves and immerse myself in this new role.

As part of my onboarding process, I was provided with articles and documentation to familiarize myself with this side of the business. While helpful, I quickly realized that my learning style required more than reading materials. I'm a hands-on learner type of gal. A person who thrives by getting out in the field, observing operations, and engaging directly with the work. Sitting at a desk for hours each day, reading through articles, left me feeling disconnected from the tangible aspects of the role. I needed to understand how things worked at their core, not just in theory but in practice.

Eager to deepen my understanding, I asked for opportunities to engage in more hands-on experiences. I envisioned shadowing team members, participating in field activities, and observing processes in real-time. However, my requests were often met with hesitance. When I expressed these thoughts during one-on-one meetings, the response given caught me off guard: "You only need to know just enough to be dangerous." At first, I wasn't sure what to make of that statement. Was it meant to encourage focus? Or was it a way of saying I didn't need the full picture?

Either way, it left me wondering how deep my role was really supposed to go. I wanted to understand the full scope of my position and the purpose I served on the team. My curiosity and eagerness to dive deeper didn't seem to be met with enthusiasm. Instead of opening doors, it felt like I was being subtly pushed to stay in a smaller box than I had expected. I started wondering how I fit into the bigger picture. I was eager to contribute but wasn't sure if I was being positioned to thrive or just to fill a seat. I wanted to do more and make an impact on the team. But at that moment, I felt unchallenged, and unfulfilled.

THE DONUT TRAP:
WHEN SEEKING SUPPORT
BECOMES A CHALLENGE

As weeks turned into months, frustration started marinating in my soul like an over-seasoned pot of collard greens. I was eager—hungry even—to contribute, bring value, and actually do something impactful. But instead of opportunities, I kept getting what felt like the corporate version of "We see you, but not really." A polite pat on the back, a calendar full of "Let's circle back", and "This is great work!" But y'all, these doors were NOT opening! And let me be clear, you can only sit on the waiting list for so long before you start building your own way."

I voiced my concerns, hoping for clarity or, at the very least, some action items. Instead, my enthusiasm seemed to widen the gap rather than bridge it. I started to wonder—was my drive being seen as ambition or annoyance? Was wanting to learn more being misread as "doing too much"?

During one of our one-on-one meetings, I was asked what I enjoyed most about my role. I paused, searching for any silver lining, and blurted out "That I get to show up to work, in style." Yep, that was my answer. Because listen—if I was going to be underutilized, I was at least going to be underutilized in style! Every day was my personal runway. I know it sounds bad, but honestly, I was reaching for anything positive to say. I wanted projects. I wanted growth. I wanted leadership to actually see my potential. Instead, I was front and center

for a leadership style that saw me as "present" but not necessarily capable.

DONUTS AND DYNAMICS:
NAVIGATING LEADERSHIP CHALLENGES

Behind closed doors, the mood was all venting and frustration—complete with dramatic sighs and midday meltdowns about how unbearable the job was. But in public? Oh, it was all polished smiles, over-the-top nods, and enough "That's great!" and "We love that!" to fill a corporate bingo card. Keeping their name spotless seemed to be priority number one—even if it meant a few people (*read: me*) got casually tossed into the office traffic. And trust me, it wasn't just a gentle nudge under the bus. I got rolled over, reversed on, and left with tire tracks like a speed bump during rush hour traffic.

And let's not forget the greatest single on the corporate playlist: *"I just want to see your growth and development."*

Now, I wanted to believe it—I really did. But after hearing it on repeat without any action to match, it started to sound more like a hopeful chorus than a real plan.

It wasn't mentorship—it was a well-packaged promise with no roadmap. And while I kept showing up, ready to grow, I couldn't help but wonder if the words were more comforting to say than they were ever meant to be lived out.

Now, let's be clear—I wasn't looking for a work bestie. I wanted an effective leader that would challenge me, coach me, and help me level up. Instead, what did I get?

DONUTS!

And not the good kind. Not the warm, melt-in-your-mouth *Krispy Kreme* kind that makes you forget your problems for 30 seconds. No, no. I got the "I-have-no-idea-how-to-lead-so-here's-a-box-of-glazed-carb-apologies" kind.

Donuts are cute, but they don't build careers.

THE FINAL STRAW
(A.K.A. THE MOMENT I KNEW I WAS DONE)

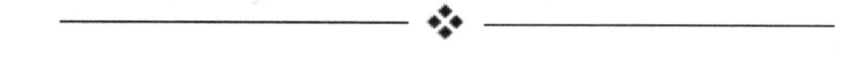

Then came the moment that sealed my decision to mentally pack my bags.

My daughter was heading to Orlando for her first solo trip, and I asked to leave a little early to help her pack. The response? "People are always watching, especially senior leadership."

Wait, watching WHAT? Me making sure my child had toothpaste? Were they secretly betting on whether I'd forget to pack socks? Was this some kind of bizarre leadership test I missed in the employee handbook?

Now, I have heard some ridiculous things in corporate spaces, but this? This was peak nonsense. Since when did making sure my child had underwear and socks require a performance review?

That comment felt like a slap in the face. Like prioritizing my daughter for two hours suddenly meant I was unfit for leadership. Spoiler alert: *It didn't.*

I hit them with the fakest, most corporate-approved smile I could muster and bit my tongue so hard I was shocked I didn't need stitches. But, y'all, my inner dialogue? It was a full-blown Netflix special—drama, comedy, and a little bit of suspense all rolled into one!"

That moment right there? It was the last straw. Their idea of leadership and what I needed were not just miles apart—they were in completely different time zones.

I needed leadership that understood balance and trust. Not someone who thought me leaving early to pack a bag was a crisis. And let's be real—I definitely didn't need a "leader" who thought that handing me a donut could fix everything.

Because, if donuts could solve leadership failures, every donut shop in America would be running Fortune 500 companies now.

DROWNING IN DONUTS:
FINDING MYSELF IN CHAOS

As time passed, I barely recognized myself. The vibrant, confident Marquetta—the one who once lit up the room with her energy—was fading. I felt like my personal brand, something my grandparents had ingrained in me, was crumbling like a stale forgotten biscuit. I wasn't Marquetta T. Hemphill anymore; I was just surviving.

My confidence nosedived. I questioned everything—my abilities, my purpose, my worth. It felt like I was under a microscope, except instead of being nurtured, I was being nitpicked. My work was overlooked, my value dismissed, and to top it off, I was excluded from the very projects that could help me grow. And then came the words that hit like a gut punch:

- *"Your previous leaders said you were amazing, so why aren't you showing that here?"*

- *"If you put as much energy into your job as you do into those external networks, you'd be great!"*

Excuse me? Say what now?! So, let me get this straight: I was being criticized for trying to build my career outside the company walls because y'all weren't giving me a seat at the table inside? Make it make sense.

It was like trying to run a marathon while someone kept moving the finish line—exhausting, disheartening, and downright infuriating. I felt trapped, suffocated. Like I was curled up in a dark closet with no light, no windows, and no way out. And y'all, I won't even lie—some days, it felt like I was losing myself entirely.

But then, in the middle of all this mess, a flicker of light appeared: I was assigned an intern.

This intern was ambitious, eager, and ready to take over the world—everything I admired, and everything I felt like I was losing in myself. Mentoring my intern became my escape, my purpose, my lifeline. I was determined to be the kind of leader for them that I desperately needed for myself.

We worked tirelessly for weeks, sharpening presentation skills, refining the narrative, and rehearsing until every detail was flawless. When the big day arrived for the project presentation, y'all, it was a masterclass in delivery! Walking into that room with undeniable confidence, the stage was owned from the very first word. And by the time the final word was spoken, the audience erupted into applause—a full standing ovation. A whole standing ovation! And just like that, the spark inside me reignited. But of course, just when I thought I could have one moment of joy, I received a message that read:

"The presentation was okay, but it was... different."

What. Does. That. Even. Mean?! Different like… incredible? Different like… *so good it got a standing ovation*? Because if by "different," that text meant *phenomenal*, then sure, I guess we agree!

But let's be real—"different" wasn't meant as a compliment. What was really being said, without being said, was that the presentation didn't fit into the familiar, comfortable mold they expected. You know, the kind of "different" that makes some folks uneasy when excellence shows up wrapped in culture, confidence, and charisma. Too much flavor. Too much authenticity. Too much of everything that made it powerful, engaging, and—let's be honest—a whole lot better than the usual lifeless PowerPoint snooze-fests. And somehow, *that* was the problem.

Y'all, I swear, every time the sun peeked through the clouds, there was always someone ready with an umbrella, a raincoat, and a whole hurricane warning. It was like playing a game of double dutch where the ropes kept getting snatched mid-jump. Just when you think you're about to hit your stride—BAM!—here comes another *conveniently vague* critique, trying to dim the shine. But see, what they failed to realize was—we don't dim, we *glow*!

But here's the shift.

For the first time, I realized something huge: My intern's success wasn't defined by one person's inability to see it. And neither was mine.

That day, I learned an invaluable lesson: storms will come, people will try to dull your shine, but their opinions don't define your worth. Watching my intern thrive reminded me of what I was capable of—even in the wrong environment.

And just like that, I knew: *it was time to shake off the negativity and start chasing the sun again.*

FROM DONUTS TO DESTINY:
A DREAM, A SONG, AND A BREAKTHROUGH

I found myself praying harder than ever before. *"God, why am I here? What am I supposed to learn from this? What is it that You want me to see?"* I was desperate, y'all—desperate for answers, clarity, and some reassurance that this storm had a purpose. The weight of my situation felt unbearable, like I was sinking deeper into something I could not escape. I felt trapped, suffocated, and utterly lost, with no idea how to move forward.

One day, during a conversation with my mentor, I finally admitted, "I'm tired. I don't understand why I keep going through this." He listened patiently before dropping one of his classic metaphors—this mentor of mine, let me tell you, has a way with metaphors that could rival any English teacher. (Honestly, I think that is his true calling).

He said to me, *"Sometimes life feels like being trapped in a closed room. You're in there, and it's hot—Mississippi summer heat hot. You're wearing a turtleneck, you're sweating, it's stuffy, and the air is so thick you can barely breathe. Then, just when you think you can't take it anymore, you notice a window. It's hard to lift at first, but you keep trying. Little by little, you manage to open it. A breeze starts flowing through, cooling you off, letting you breathe again. It's not instant, but it's happening. The relief is coming."*

That metaphor hit me straight in the gut. He reminded me that my prayers weren't going unheard—I just had to trust that **change was already in motion**.

He used that metaphor to remind me that God hears me. He said, "You've been crying out, and now you have to trust God. Let God work." Those words, paired with his vivid analogy, gave me a sense of peace I had not felt in a long time. It reminded me that even when life feels suffocating, relief is on its way—it's just a matter of time and trust.

A couple of days later, after that conversation, I had a dream so vivid it left me completely baffled when I woke up. It wasn't just a dream, it felt like a message, a vision that shook me to my core. In this dream, I was standing in the front yard of a house, surrounded by people whose faces were blurred and unrecognizable. Suddenly, out of nowhere, a huge black rattlesnake—easily the size of a python—slithered through the grass. Its movements were slow but deliberate, and calculated, like it knew exactly what it was doing. Before I could even process what was happening, the snake wrapped itself tightly around my waist.

Strangely enough, the pressure was not overwhelming. I could feel its strength, but I wasn't afraid. And if you know me, you know this had to be a dream, because in real life? Baby, I would've been on top of somebody's roof hollering for my life!

Everyone around me bolted to the safety of the porch, running like their lives depended on it. But not me—oh no, my crazy self was planted right there in the yard. My arms stretched out like a capital "T," frozen in place. I didn't move, didn't speak. I just stood there looking like I was hitting my best runway pose (y'all know I love fashion, so even in chaos, your girl gonna make sure she is camera ready).

Then the snake's rattle began to shake—loudly. The sound was piercing and demanded my full attention. At that moment, it felt like the entire dream narrowed down to just me, the snake, and that deafening rattle. It was the only thing I could hear, the only thing I could focus on.

Out of the blue, a familiar face emerged, a calm and steady presence walking toward me. She didn't say a word or make any sudden moves, but the moment she came closer, the snake released its grip, uncoiled itself from my waist, and disappeared as quickly as it appeared. The dream ended, but its intensity stayed with me long after I woke up.

I jumped up out of my sleep and now my mind was racing. What did this mean? And why that snake? The dream stayed with me, vivid and unshakable. It was as if God was speaking to me in a way that only I could understand, showing me something I needed to see. I didn't know what the message was at the time, but I knew it was significant. That dream became a turning point, a moment that forced me to confront my fears, my faith, and the power I had within me to overcome even the tightest grip of struggle. I woke up shaken, trying to make sense of what I had just seen. What did this dream mean? Why a snake? I could not piece it together at the time, so I did what I always do when I'm confused, I prayed, then called my mom. "God, I need understanding. Show me what this dream means."

Days passed, and I kept replaying the dream in my mind. The suffocation I felt in the dream mirrored how I felt in my role—trapped and powerless. That snake wasn't just some random image; it represented the weight of my situation, the doubt, the frustration, the feeling of being stuck. But then, there was the moment of deliverance—the familiar face stepping in, and just like that, the snake was gone. That had to mean something. I held onto that image of freedom, of release, praying for the day it would manifest in my life.

Now, God knows me. He knows that I'm stubborn and that subtle hints? Yeah, they go right over my head. So, when He speaks to me, it's never quiet—it's loud, clear, and impossible to ignore. One morning, as I was driving to work, the song "It's Only a Test" by Bishop Larry Trotter dropped into my spirit. I hadn't thought about that song in years, but the second it came to mind, I knew I needed to hear it.

I queued it up, and as the melody filled my car, something in me broke. The lyrics reminded me that trials are temporary, pain has a purpose, and God never puts more on us than we can bear. I didn't just hear the words—I felt them deep in my soul. Tears streamed down my face as I drove. It wasn't just a cry—it was a release. I was sobbing, shouting, and praising all at the same time. My truck? It turned into a full-blown sanctuary.

Right there, on the highway, I had a full-on praise and worship session. I didn't care who saw me or what they thought. This? This was my breakthrough.

In that moment, I felt the chains breaking. The heaviness in my chest lifted, and I could finally breathe again. It was as if God was whispering,
"I got you, Marquetta. This is only a test, and you ARE going to pass it."

For the first time in months, I felt peace. Not because my circumstances had changed—because they hadn't. But because I knew they would change. God had heard my cries, and I believed with all my heart that my deliverance was on the way.

That day, I walked into the office with a renewed sense of purpose. My situation hadn't shifted yet, but my mindset had. I realized that sometimes, the real battle isn't external—it's internal. It's about trusting God's timing, even when you can't see the finish line. It's about holding onto faith, even when the weight of the world is pressing down on you.

And let me tell y'all—there's always that one moment when enough is enough. And for me? That moment had arrived.

Let's just say… the tension had been brewing for a while. I had been biting my tongue, staying professional, but this time, I broke my silence. Now, don't get me wrong—I didn't go full "flip tables and act a fool" mode, though every fiber of my being wanted to. (Growth, y'all—thank you, God, for growth!) But I was firm. My tone was sharp enough to cut through the tension like a hot knife through butter.

The conversation got tense. We were both standing our ground, voices firm but controlled, until eventually… silence. You know the kind— the thick, unspoken, "this ain't working" type of silence.

At that moment, I knew I was done. I had poured everything I could into this situation. I had given my best, shown up fully, and still found myself hitting a wall.

After the tension ironed out, I did what I always do when I hit my breaking point: I called my mama. She prayed for me—one of those "call-down-heaven" types of prayers that only a mama can do. Then, I called my husband to vent, because let's be real—he's my sounding board for all things stressful. But even with their support, I felt like I couldn't take another day in that environment. I was emotionally drained, spiritually depleted, and just flat-out tired. Something had to change, and it had to change fast.

Later that day, as I headed up the elevator, I ran into a friend. She knew my situation all too well, probably better than I had even shared. She leaned in and said, "I didn't get the job."

Y'all. I froze. This could only mean one thing—the position had been filled, and I already knew who got it! And in that instant, it clicked. That meant that if she didn't get the job, that meant God had answered my prayers.

And just like that, I no longer felt trapped, I could breathe! I asked her to repeat herself, and when she did, I swear I felt the heavens open right there on that elevator. I didn't even wait for her to finish explaining.

As soon as those elevator doors opened, I walked straight into the Ladies' restroom, locked myself in a stall, and just let it all out. I cried tears I didn't even know I had left. Big, ugly, snotty tears of relief and freedom. It was as if every weight I had been carrying was suddenly lifted.

I was FREE!

As soon as I could catch my breath, I grabbed my phone and called my mama. Of course, she was worried because all she heard on the other end was me hollering, *"Maaaaa, I'm free!"* Thank you, God, I'm free!" Between sobs, I explained what had happened, and my mama, being the prayer warrior she is, started praying on the spot. And then she reminded me of something that stopped me in my tracks:

"Quetta! The dream! Remember the dream!"

It hit me like a ton of bricks. The dream about the snake wrapping itself around me, only to vanish when help arrived—it was not just some random nightmare. It was confirmation. God had already shown me that this moment was coming. I wasn't stuck. I wasn't bound. I was free.

That realization washed over me like a wave. I had spent so much time questioning why I was in that place, but now I saw it clearly—I had learned what I needed to learn, and it was time to move forward. I no longer had to hold in my frustrations. I was stepping into a new chapter where my voice, my skills, and my growth mattered.

That day, I felt the full weight of my freedom. I wasn't just leaving a place where I no longer thrived. I was stepping boldly into the leader I knew I could be. The experience didn't break me; it built me. And now, I was ready to take everything I had learned and apply it to my next chapter.

With every tear, prayer, and moment of growth, I was reminded of one thing:

God always shows up. And when He does, He shows OUT.

BREAKING THE GLAZE:
LEADERSHIP AND GROWTH REFLECTIONS

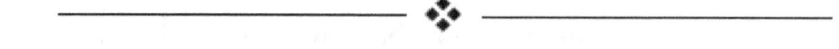

It wasn't until I started working with a new leader that I began to see value in my role. This wasn't just another manager—this was a leader who recognized my potential and made an effort to invest in me. They didn't just delegate tasks; they took the time to explain the bigger picture, showing me how my contributions fit into the organization's success. It was like a lightbulb went off. For the first time in a long time, I felt seen, valued, and heard.

With this leader, there was no guessing game. Expectations were clear, feedback was constructive, and there was a genuine sense of trust. They didn't hover or micromanage, but they were present enough to guide and support me when needed. They celebrated my wins and challenged me to step outside my comfort zone in ways that pushed me to grow. Slowly but surely, I started to find my confidence again.

One question that kept coming up from leadership was, *"Marquetta, you're clearly capable of this role, so what has been holding you back from showing your true potential?"* Without hesitation, I always answered, "Support. I needed support." And let me be clear, support is not a handout, nor is it someone doing the work for you. Support is having a leader who creates an environment where you can thrive, grow, and excel in your role.

For me, a supportive leader would have meant someone who didn't just assign tasks but invested in my development. It is about having a leader who provides clear guidance, actionable feedback, and the tools necessary to succeed. It's about someone who doesn't see questions as a threat but as an opportunity to teach and empower. Support is knowing that when you take a step forward, your leader is there to back you up, fostering growth instead of creating roadblocks.

When I think of what could have been, I imagine a leader who could have helped me navigate the challenges of my role, identify areas for growth, and celebrate my wins—big or small. There were times when I found myself facing challenges alone, questioning my decisions, and seeking clarity on my path. I longed for a leader who could guide me through the complexities of the business, someone who believed in my potential and knew how to harness it effectively.

Support is also about creating a culture of trust. It's knowing that your leader has your back, not just waiting for you to stumble so they can say, "I told you so." It's about someone who actively involves you in conversations, includes you in key decisions, and values your perspective. With that kind of support, I could have taken my role to new heights. I could have focused on driving results and making an impact instead of constantly questioning whether I was good enough.

I realized that having a supportive leader is not a luxury; it's a necessity for anyone who wants to grow and succeed. It's the foundation for confidence, innovation, and excellence in any job. And while I eventually found that strength within myself, I now strive to be the kind of leader I once needed—someone who supports, uplifts, and helps others reach their full potential. Because I know firsthand how much of a difference that can make.

FROM DONUTS TO DESTINY:
A SHIFT IN THE MAKING

Leaving behind that challenging work environment had been a blessing, but even in this new space, I couldn't shake the feeling that there was something more waiting for me. It wasn't about being unhappy—I wasn't miserable anymore—but there was this itch, this nudge deep in my spirit that kept saying, "This isn't it." I was working, smiling, and doing what needed to be done, but mentally and spiritually, I was somewhere else.

I started interviewing for new roles, putting myself out there and praying hard. I'd make it to the top three candidates, only to hear the dreaded words: "We've decided to go in another direction." Y'all, let me tell you, that phrase will humble you real quick! I kept pushing, but nothing was working. My spirit felt restless, and I began to check out. I would show up physically, but mentally, I was gone.

During this time, my husband became my rock. I remember sitting with him one night and saying, "Babe, let's make sure we're financially prepared for anything." I didn't know why, but I felt like something was coming." It's just something that I felt was about to happen deep down in my "Sha-na-na." I masked it under the uncertainty of the economy, but deep down, I knew this wasn't just about external factors. God was stirring something in me, and while I didn't know what it was, I could feel it in my gut. Something was coming.

My mom and husband were my lifelines. Every morning on my drive to work, they would answer the phone and listen to me vent. Bless their hearts, they deserve medals for putting up with me during this time. I was not bitter, but I was frustrated. I wanted more, and I couldn't figure out what that "more" was. The one thing that kept me sane was mentoring. Pouring into others gave me joy and purpose. As my mentors used to say, "The best way to thank me is to pour into others what I've poured into you." And that's exactly what I did.

But still, something felt... off.

I remember one morning showing up to work wearing an all-gray pant-suit. Now, let me set the scene for you. Anyone who knows me knows I live for colors! Bold, vibrant, joyful hues—that's my signature. Me in gray? That's like a peacock walking around featherless. It was so out of character that even my coworkers did double-takes. One of them even asked, "Marquetta, are you okay? This outfit doesn't look like *you* at all." It was that bad! Looking back, I realized that the grey suit was more than just a wardrobe choice—it was a reflection of how I was feeling inside. Something was just not right, and even my fashion couldn't hide it. But looking back, that gray pantsuit was prophetic. It was preparation for what was coming next.

That same morning, I got to my desk and tried to settle into work, but something felt heavy. I was mentally checked out, more than usual on this particular day. And then, at exactly 11:13 a.m., I heard the word: SHIFT. Clear as day, loud in my spirit. "Lord," I whispered, "what does that mean? Is today the day? Am I getting the call, the promotion, the breakthrough?"

And then, out of nowhere, I felt the urge to pack up my desk. Y'all, it didn't make any sense, but I couldn't shake it. I started grabbing my things, quietly boxing everything off my desk. The crazy part? I managed to pack up my entire desk without a single person noticing.

Stealth mode activated! I took the boxes to my truck and shared with a coworker that God had told me to pack up. I didn't understand it, I didn't know why, but it was just something that had to be done at that moment.

For weeks, I carried this feeling in my spirit. Every day, I would tell my mom and husband, "Something's coming. I don't know what it is, but I can feel it." The anticipation was almost unbearable. Imagine knowing a storm is on the horizon but not being able to see the clouds yet. That's how I felt—stuck between faith and the unknown.

Three weeks passed. On Monday morning, I dragged myself to work, going through the motions as usual. By noon, I could not take it anymore and left work early. Later that evening, a meeting invite popped up on my calendar for 9 a.m. the next day. Something about it felt...off. I told my husband, "This meeting doesn't feel right." The meeting invite came from someone I hadn't had a one-on-one with in months. Why now? What could this be about? My mom, who knows I have a sharp mouth said, "Lord, let me pray because this child of mine will pop off at the drop of a dime." Yea, I am one of those, if something makes me feel some type of way, you will know about it in that moment, but y'all, I'm working on it – my Christian walk is being refined daily, better yet, hourly!

The next morning, I walked into the meeting room, where the meeting organizer, an HR manager, and VP were already seated, waiting for me. Let me tell you—my mom must have been praying nonstop because, to my surprise, a wave of calmness settled over me as I took my seat. They started with the usual polished corporate phrases: *"Due to business needs," "You've been such an asset," "Your personality shines so bright."* But I saw right through it. I already knew where this was going. And then, just as expected, they delivered the news: *"Your role is being eliminated."*

Now, most people would panic, but me? I wanted to shout, "Hallelujah!" I had prayed for this moment, and here it was. They handed me a severance package, and I couldn't have been happier. As I drove home, I couldn't help but think—Man, I wish they had told me this before I made that long drive this morning!"

As I left the building for the last time, I felt a weight lift off my shoulders. My chains were broken, and I was free! I called my mom, and through tears of joy, I said, "Maaaaa, I'm free! Thank you, Jesus, I'm free!" My mom, in her infinite wisdom, reminded me of the snake dream again. "Quetta," she said, "God showed you this. He's been preparing you."

She was right. God had answered my prayers, but not on my timeline—on His. This wasn't the end. It was the beginning. A *shift*. The next chapter of my journey was unfolding, and I knew it was time to step into my calling fully.

And just like that, *"I Got Donuts"* would be born.

THE LESSON I LEARNED

Y'all, let me break it down—the biggest lesson I've learned from these donut-filled detours is that growth isn't some sweet, powdered sugar stroll. It's messy. It's sticky. It's like biting into a jelly donut with no napkins in sight. But you know what? Every crumb of that mess **is absolutely worth it.**

Resilience isn't just about surviving the donuts tossed your way. It's about catching those stale ones mid-air, tossing them like yesterday's leftovers, and strutting into the bakery of life like, *"Alright, what's fresh today?"*—and doing it all while rocking a power blazer and heels so bad they have folks whispering, *"Oh, Sis did NOT come to play!"* Because let's be real—when you look good, you feel good, and when you feel good, even the crustiest, over-glazed nonsense can't dim your shine.

But here's the real deal: resilience means standing firm in who you are, even when the world tries to glaze over your greatness. If you're sitting around waiting for someone to serve you the perfect leadership opportunity on a silver platter, you'll end up like me—staring at an empty donut box wondering, *"Is this all there is?"* Sometimes, you have to bake your own success, even if the kitchen gets a little messy.

Leadership? Baby, listen—it's so much more than walking in with the biggest box of donuts and expecting applause. True leadership is about filling the room with substance, not sugar. It's about being the yeast in the dough—helping others rise—and shaking off the crumbs of bad leadership to say, *"We deserve better, and we're going to make it better."*

Here's the biggest takeaway: perspective is your sprinkles. Once I stopped focusing on the donuts that were missing and started asking, *"How can I use what I have to make something amazing?"* everything shifted. It's like stepping into a kitchen thinking you have nothing, only to realize you've got all the ingredients to whip up something incredible.

And the humor of it all? Life will serve you moments where you bite into a donut, only to find it's hollow inside. But instead of staying stuck in disappointment, you laugh, you learn, and you keep it moving—because staying stuck? That's definitely NOT the vibe.

POURING INTO OTHERS

One of the greatest lessons I've learned is that my journey—every trial, triumph, and donut moment—was never just for me. Every challenge was shaping me to guide and uplift others. I have grown into the kind of mentor I once needed—someone who sees the spark in people and pours into them unapologetically.

When I mentor, I don't just share advice; I share my heart. I want people to know they're not alone, and that success isn't about squeezing into someone else's mold. They can be bold, vibrant, and fully themselves—and still rise to the top.

My confidence? It comes from knowing I've been through the **FIRE.** I've been stretched, tested, and refined like dough under pressure—and I'm still standing. No, scratch that—I'm thriving. I have risen, just like the perfect donut dough when the timing and ingredients are just right. And now, I'm walking boldly in my purpose, sprinkling wisdom and success into the lives of others as I climb.

I've learned that resilience is the **yeast** that helps us rise, purpose is the **filling** that keeps us whole, and sharing joy with others is the **glaze** that makes life sweeter. True leadership isn't about tossing a box of donuts on the counter and calling it a day. It's about making sure everyone gets a piece—while empowering them to bake their own batch of greatness.

STANDING IN MY TRUTH

Through it all—the highs, the lows, and the moments of doubt—I have come to love the woman I see in the mirror. I love the vibrant, ambitious, unapologetically Mississippi-bred woman I was always meant to be. I no longer shrink myself to fit into someone else's narrative. Instead, I stand tall in my truth because my authenticity… That's my superpower.

So here I am, **Marquetta Toshe**, a woman who refuses to be boxed into roles that don't reflect her true self. A woman who knows her worth, walks boldly in her purpose, and thrives in helping others see their own light. I am the cheerleader who celebrates both the big wins and the small victories because every step matters, and every milestone deserves to be acknowledged.

I believe everyone has a light within them waiting to shine. My mission is to help others uncover that light, even when the world tries to dim it. Whether through mentorship, leadership, or simply being a listening ear, I pour into others what has been poured into me. Because success isn't just about reaching the top—it's about bringing others with you, cheering them on, and proving that they, too, can rise to greatness.

Because, let's be real—life might throw you donuts, but you…

You're about to bake something legendary.

WHAT'S WITH DONUTS?

You know by now that *I Got Donuts* is not about glazed treats or coffee outings—though, let's be real, a perfectly made maple bacon donut will always have a place in my heart. No, donuts in this context are so much more. They are a metaphor for what I have seen, felt, and experienced throughout my journey in the workplace. Donuts represent leadership and actions that *look* sweet on the outside but leave you empty on the inside. They are hollow gestures—momentary distractions from deeper issues that never truly get solved.

For professionals navigating the workplace—regardless of background, race, or culture—donuts show up in countless forms. Maybe it's the *mentor* who says all the right things but never follows through with meaningful guidance. Or the so-called *promotion* that piles on extra responsibilities but conveniently skips the title, salary, or recognition. Perhaps it's being given *just enough responsibility to be dangerous*—trusted to do the work but never equipped with the tools, resources, or opportunities to truly thrive. Sound familiar? These are the donuts, and trust me, they're not the kind you want.

Donuts are easy. They're sweet, quick, and require little effort. They get handed out as a substitute for what really matters—genuine support, intentional leadership, and meaningful growth. But here's the thing: donuts, as tempting as they may seem in the moment, are never enough to sustain you. They don't bridge the gap between where you are and where you want to be. They're empty gestures, masking the lack of real investment in your potential.

I have seen donuts handed out in many forms throughout my career.

- A boss who calls you *valuable* but never advocates for you when it counts.

- A team meeting filled with motivational platitudes but no real action plans.

- A leader who brings donuts to the table instead of solutions, strategies, or a genuine commitment to your growth.

Recognizing these donuts for what they are is a critical step in reclaiming your power and defining your own journey.

Here's the truth:

Donuts do not reflect your worth. Let me say that again—**donuts do NOT reflect your worth**. Those hollow gestures are not a reflection of your capabilities, your contributions, or your potential. They are a reflection of leadership that lacks the depth to truly see and support you. And once you recognize that, you stop internalizing it. You stop questioning your value because of someone else's inability to lead effectively.

But this isn't just about *calling out* the donuts—it's about using them as catalysts for growth. It's about demanding substance over surface, authenticity over appearances, and growth over temporary fixes. It's about creating your own opportunities, building your own legacy, and ensuring that *you* define your success—not anyone else.

When I stopped letting the donuts hold me back, I started using them as fuel. Every hollow gesture became a reminder of what I *truly* deserved: real investment, real opportunities, and leadership that not only recognizes my potential, and helps to unlock it. And now, I'm here to tell you—you can do the same.

You don't have to settle for donuts. You don't have to accept surface-level leadership or empty promises. You have the power to demand better, build your brand, and chart your own path. This is *your* story to write, *your* journey to take, and *your* shift to experience. And trust me—when you rise above the donuts, the view is worth it.

So, the next time someone walks into the room with a box of donuts, ask yourself: *Is this a genuine offering, or is it a distraction?* Then decide how you will turn that moment into a stepping stone for your growth. Because at the end of the day, it's not about the donuts—it's about you.

Your value. Your journey. Your success.

And that? Is far greater than any temporary fix someone tries to hand you. Let the donuts remind you of that—and then go claim what is rightfully yours.

The Roadmap: From Donuts to Destiny

This section is your guide, your playbook, and your career survival kit—think of it as your GPS for navigating the twists and turns of your professional journey without getting lost in the glaze. It is about recognizing challenges, learning from obstacles, and carving your own path forward. Whether you are just starting out, climbing the ladder, or contemplating a career shift, this guide is for you.

But before we dive in, let's set some intentions. Grab a notebook, and your favorite pen, then get ready to put in the work. This isn't just a book; it's a conversation, a collaboration, and a call to action.

Navigating Through the Assortment of Donuts

Alright y'all, let us get one thing straight. When I say, "I Got Donuts," I am not just talking about pastries. Don't get me wrong, I will happily take a maple bacon donut any day of the week. But this is deeper than a box of sugary treats. The "I Got Donuts" metaphor is about leadership—or, more specifically, the lack of it.

It is about those hollow gestures that look good on the surface but fail to nourish or sustain anyone in the long run.

Let me break it down for you. Leadership—real leadership—is about investment. It is about people. It is about rolling up your sleeves and pouring into your team so they can grow, thrive, and shine. But too often in the workplace, I've seen a parade of donuts.

These are the superficial fixes, the "look busy" strategies, and the performative efforts designed to give the appearance of care without any of the work that comes with real leadership.

And here is the kicker—these donuts come in different flavors. Yes, leadership has its own donut menu. Let me introduce you to some of the usual flavors:

- **The Glazed Donut Leader**

This is the classic. They show up looking polished and sweet, but there is nothing beyond the shiny surface. These are the leaders who smile in meetings, talk about teamwork, and drop in for the occasional chitchat but leave you high and dry when you need real support. The glaze wears off fast when you realize there is no substance underneath.

- **The Jelly-Filled Donut Leader**

Oh, this one. You never quite know what you're going to get. These leaders are unpredictable. One day, they are supportive, praising you in front of the team. The next, they are nitpicking and ghosting you when it is time to deliver on promises. Like jelly filling, their leadership style is messy and leaves you wondering, "What just happened?"

- **The Powdered Donut Leader**

These leaders are…well, messy. They might mean well, but their lack of organization creates chaos everywhere they go. Working under them feels like cleaning up powdered sugar—no matter how hard you try, the mess keeps spreading.

- **The Maple Bacon Donut Leader**

This leader tries way too hard to be everything at once. Sweet? Check. Savory? Check. Overwhelming? Definitely. They are all over the place, piling on complexity without any clear direction. You leave every interaction thinking, "Was that supposed to help me?" Because I'm more confused than before.

- **The Donut Hole Leader**

Do not let their small size fool you—this one is a big deal. These leaders are barely there. They delegate everything, dodge accountability, and are impossible to find when things go sideways. They are the donut holes of leadership: small, empty, and easy to overlook.

Why Does This Assortment of Donuts Matter?

Now, you ask – Marquetta, why are you breaking this down? Because recognizing these "donuts" is the first step toward taking back your power. When you can identify these hollow gestures for what they are, you stop internalizing them. You stop thinking, "Maybe it's me," and start realizing, "No, this is them."

The goal is not just to spot the donuts but to rise above them. When you understand what real leadership looks like—investment, authenticity, and accountability, you can demand it for yourself. You can set boundaries, build your brand, and work toward environments where you are genuinely supported and empowered.

Now that we have unpacked the many flavors of "I Got Donuts" leadership, it is time to get personal. If you are anything like me, you have probably had moments in your career where you knew something was off. You saw the glazed smiles, felt the powdered chaos, or maybe even got stuck cleaning up the jelly mess left behind by someone else. You have encountered the donuts—you just may not have had a name for them until now.

Guess what? Recognizing donuts is not about pointing fingers or holding grudges. It is about gaining clarity. It is about understanding the patterns, behaviors, and empty gestures that have left you feeling stuck, unfulfilled, or even invisible in your workplace. And once you can clearly identify these moments, you can start taking steps to shift your focus from what is not working for you to what you need to thrive.

Grab your pen, your notebook, or whatever helps you gather your thoughts, because it is time to turn those fluff-filled signs into something real and satisfying for your success.

EXERCISE ONE:
RECOGNIZING THE DONUTS
FOR WHAT THEY ARE

"Not every donut is worth the bite—recognize what is hollow and what truly feeds your growth."

Think about your current (or past) workplace. Ask yourself:

- Have I been given tasks or opportunities without clear guidance or support'?

- Have I ever felt like I was being kept "just dangerous enough" but not allowed to thrive?

- Have I seen gestures (like donuts) that look good on the outside but don't address the real needs of the team?

Reflection Prompt: Write down three examples of when you encountered *donuts* in your career journey. How did those situations make you feel? Did you speak up? Why or why not?

Recognizing donuts for what they are is not about holding on to bitterness or playing the blame game, it's about clarity. It's about seeing things for what they truly are, not what they are dressed up to be. When you identify the hollow gestures, the acts, and the empty promises in your workplace, you gain the power to stop internalizing them as a reflection of your worth or abilities. Instead, you can look at them for what they are: distractions, placeholders, or surface-level attempts at leadership.

When you recognize the donuts in your workplace, it is important to avoid certain distractions:

- **Do not dwell on them:** Overanalyzing every hollow gesture can drain your energy and keep you stuck in a cycle of frustration. Acknowledge them, but do not let them consume you.

- **Do not internalize them:** The donuts are not a reflection of your worth or value. They are symptoms of leadership gaps, not your capabilities.

- Do not assume malice: Not every leader serving donuts is doing so intentionally. Sometimes they lack the tools, experience, or awareness to lead effectively. This does not mean you should excuse it, but it helps to approach the situation with a constructive mindset.

What to Do Instead - Clarity gives you the ability to refocus. Instead of spending time and energy waiting for the support, guidance, or recognition that may never come, start building for yourself:

- *Shift your focus*: Stop dwelling on what is not being offered and start identifying what you need to grow. Ask yourself, what skills do I want to develop? What opportunities align with my goals?

- *Find your village*: Seek out mentors, sponsors, and allies who genuinely invest in you and want to see you succeed. These are the people who will help you navigate beyond the donuts.

- ***Be your own advocate***: Speak up about what you need and want. Clearly communicate your goals and the support required to achieve them. Remember, people cannot support you if they do not know what you are working toward.

Coaching Your Leader

Sometimes, your leader may not even realize they are serving donuts instead of providing true support. It is perfectly acceptable, and even beneficial to coach your leader. Yes, you read that right. Coaching your leader is not about being disrespectful or assuming superiority; it is about fostering a productive relationship that benefits everyone.

- *Be constructive*: Instead of focusing on what is missing, frame your needs in a way that highlights mutual benefits. For example, *"I believe I could contribute more effectively if I had regular check-ins for feedback and direction."*

- *Lead with curiosity*: Ask questions that encourage your leader to reflect on their approach. *"What do you think are the biggest areas for my growth, and how can we work together to develop those?"*

- *Offer solutions*: If you notice a gap in leadership, suggest actionable ways to address it. This could be asking for specific resources, proposing new initiatives, or requesting mentorship opportunities.

Lesson: The key here is to use this clarity to reframe your mindset. You are not stuck because of the donuts being served; you are stuck if you allow those donuts to define your journey. Once you understand that the surface-level gestures are just that—on the surface—you free yourself to dig deeper, build substance, and define your own success.

This lesson is not about walking away bitter or upset. It is about walking away better.

Better equipped to navigate your career

Better prepared to advocate for yourself

Better positioned to create opportunities that align with your purpose and potential.

Recognizing donuts is step one. Step two is building a strategy to rise above them, and yes, sometimes even helping the donut-makers realize they can do better. That shift is where your real power begins.

EXERCISE TWO:
LEARNING FROM THE DONUTS
AND IDENTIFY THE GAP

Donuts are not just empty gestures; they are signals flashing brightly, letting you know where something is missing. They highlight gaps in leadership, overlooked opportunities, or the absence of genuine support. Instead of letting these moments frustrate or dishearten you, what if you flipped the script? What if you used these donut moments as a guide to build something better for yourself?

Each donut moment—every time you were given a task without clear guidance, passed over for a promotion, or handed a hollow gesture instead of real support—contains valuable lessons. These moments can teach you about your values, clarify your needs, and show you where change is necessary. The key is to not let them define you. Instead, use them as stepping stones to take control of your career and personal growth.

Take a moment to revisit the examples you wrote down in Exercise One. Let us dig a little deeper. Ask yourself the following questions for each situation:

What was missing?

- Was it mentorship from a leader who could have guided you?

- Was it transparency, like understanding the "why" behind decisions?

- Was it an opportunity where your contributions were over-looked, and your potential untapped?

- Maybe it was recognition or inclusion, where your value and voice were minimized?

What did you need at that moment?

- Would clear feedback have helped you grow and improve?

- Would a mentor have given you the tools to navigate challenges and seize opportunities?

- Did you need someone to advocate for you or create a space where you felt heard and supported?

Reflection Prompt: Now, let us take it a step further. Think about how you can begin to fill those gaps for yourself:

- If mentorship was missing, who outside your immediate circle can you reach out to for guidance? Remember, mentors can be found in surprising places.

- If opportunity was lacking, can you create one? For instance, pitch a project that aligns with your strengths and showcases your skills.

- If feedback was unclear, can you seek it proactively? Have a conversation with your leader to understand where you stand and how you can grow.

The goal is not to dwell on what was missing but to identify actionable ways to move forward. By reflecting on these gaps, you gain clarity about what you need and can start taking steps to fill those spaces intentionally.

Lesson: Here's the hard truth, unfortunately, donuts will always show up in some form. But they do not have to define you. They are not roadblocks meant to stop you. They are roadmaps that reveal the areas where you can grow and demand better for yourself.

Recognizing donuts is not about bitterness or resentment. It is about clarity and empowerment. It is about understanding your worth and refusing to settle for less than you deserve. Each donut moment is an invitation to reflect, adjust, and take ownership of your journey.

Roll up your sleeves and get to work. Use those donuts as fuel for your growth. Let them remind you of your resilience, your potential, and your ability to create opportunities for yourself. The next time a donut shows up in your career, you will not just recognize it, you will know exactly what to do with it.

EXERCISE THREE: EXPERIENCING YOUR SHIFT

"The Power of the Shift"

Now that you have taken a close look at the gaps—the donuts in your journey—it is time to flip the script entirely. Recognizing what was missing is just the beginning. What truly changes your outlook is how you respond. That response is what I call "the shift."

Shifts are not just about external changes like getting a new title, moving to a different department, or landing a better opportunity. While those things are great, real shifts start inside. They are about waking up your worth, owning your narrative, and committing yourself to change even if it means starting with the small, quiet steps no one else can see. Basically, shift your mindset!

This is where the journey becomes personal and powerful. It is not about waiting for someone to hand you a donut anymore. It is about baking your own, with all the flavors and fillings you deserve. So, let us move forward from identifying the gaps to building the bridge that gets you to your ideal professional life.

A shift is not just about external change; it is about an internal awakening. It is recognizing when something no longer serves you, understanding what you need, and taking intentional steps toward your next chapter.

Shifts happen when you decide that where you are is not where you are meant to stay.

Reflect on Your Current Situation:

- Take a step back and evaluate where you are right now. What about your current role or environment feels out of sync? What excites you, energizes you, and makes you feel alive? On the flip side, what drains you, frustrates you, or leaves you feeling undervalued? Write these down in as much detail as possible. Do not hold back—this is your moment of honesty with yourself.

Define Your Shifts:

- Once you have reflected, pinpoint three specific areas in your professional life that you want to change or improve. Maybe you want to develop a skill that sets you apart. Perhaps you are ready to pursue a leadership role or step into a space where your voice is valued. Or maybe it is time to shift your mindset, shedding self-doubt and embracing confidence. Be clear and intentional about what you want to address.

Take Actionable Steps:

- For each of the three areas you identified, write down one small, actionable step you can take today. It does not have to be monumental—it just has to move you closer to your shift.

  - *Example 1*: If you want better mentorship, reach out to someone you admire and ask for a quick chat. You will be surprised how many leaders are willing to have a conversation with you.

  - *Example 2:* If you are craving a new skill, commit to researching a class or starting a free online course.

Learning something new is always a good route and can shift your focus to what is happening now while preparing for your future.

○ *Example 3:* If you are seeking clarity, set aside time to journal or meditate on your career goals.

Reflection Prompt: What does your ideal career look like? Close your eyes and picture yourself thriving. What are you doing? Who are you working with? How does it feel to wake up and love what you do? Write it all down in vivid detail. The more specific you are, the clearer your path to that vision becomes.

Lesson: The thing about shifts: they do not happen overnight. They take preparation, patience, and persistence. It is not just about waiting for the stars to align; it is about preparing yourself mentally, emotionally, and spiritually so that when the shift comes, you are ready to step into it with confidence.

It is also important to remember that shifts are not linear. You may take two steps forward and one step back, but every movement is progress. The key is to stay consistent and committed to the vision you have for yourself.

This is your journey, your shift, your moment to turn everything you have learned, including the lessons from those donuts, into actionable growth. Let us embrace the power of the shift and move into where we take what we have learned and turn it into a thriving roadmap for the future.

Exercise Four:
Building Your Roadmap

"Create Your Career GPS"

Now that you have started preparing for your shift and identifying areas in your career that need change, it is time to take those reflections and turn them into an actionable plan. This is where you stop reacting to the circumstances around you and start proactively shaping your future. Navigating your career, especially as someone from an underrepresented background, is not just about hard work. It is about strategy, clarity, and having a solid roadmap. Think of this as your personal GPS, guiding you through the twists and turns of corporate spaces. The good news? You are in the driver's seat, and now it is time to chart your path forward.

A career without a clear direction can feel like wandering through a maze with no end in sight. Every opportunity and challenge can leave you questioning, "Am I on the right path?"

That is why building your roadmap is essential; it helps you stay focused on where you are going and ensures every step you take gets you closer to your destination. Let us break this down into bite-sized batches:

Define Your Destination

Before you start your journey, you need to know where you are going. What does success look like for you? Take a moment to craft a clear vision statement that inspires and motivates you.

- Ask yourself:

  o What kind of leader or professional do I want to be?

  o What values do I want to embody in my career?

  o What kind of legacy do I want to leave behind?

  o **Example:** "I want to lead a team where everyone feels supported, heard, and valued."

This vision becomes your signature recipe, guiding every ingredient you add to your journey moving forward.

Mark Your Milestones

Big goals can feel overwhelming, so break them down into smaller, achievable milestones. Think of these as the checkpoints on your roadmap.

- What are the skills, experiences, or opportunities you need to reach your ultimate goal?

- **Example:**

  o "Within the next six months, I will improve my public speaking skills by joining a Toastmasters group."

  o "Within the next year, I will seek a leadership training program to strengthen my management abilities."

Each milestone should feel challenging, yet attainable.

Identify Your Allies

You are not meant to navigate this journey alone. A strong support system of mentors, sponsors, and peers can open doors you did not even know existed.

- Who in your network inspires you? Who has the knowledge or connections to guide you?

Reflection Point:

- Reach out to someone you admire on LinkedIn and ask for a 15-minute coffee chat.

- Join professional groups or communities where you can meet like-minded individuals.

Allies are like sprinkles. They add the extra flavor, support, and spark you need to keep thriving and moving forward.

Set Boundaries

One of the most important lessons in building your career is learning what to say no to. Not every task, role, or opportunity will align with your goals, and that is okay.

- What tasks or responsibilities are draining your energy and pulling you away from your bigger vision?

- **Example:**

  o "I cannot take on this project right now, but I'd be happy to assist once my current tasks are complete."

Setting boundaries is not about being difficult; it is about protecting your time, energy, and focus for what truly matters.

Celebrating Wins

Progress, no matter how small, deserves recognition. Celebrating your achievements keeps you motivated and reminds you that you are moving in the right direction.

- How can you reward yourself for reaching milestones, both big and small?

- **Example:** Treat yourself to a new outfit, new shoes, or a day off after completing a challenging project. Go spoil yourself!

Acknowledging your wins, even the small ones, builds momentum for your journey ahead.

Lesson: Your career roadmap is not a one-size-fits-all template. It is yours to customize, adjust, and refine as you grow. Some detours and delays may come, but with a clear destination, marked milestones, and the right support system, you will stay on track.

Now, as we move forward, we will explore how to use what you have learned and turn it into actionable growth. Let us keep building one intentional step at a time.

EXERCISE FIVE:
POURING INTO OTHERS

"The Legacy of Leadership"

True success is not just about climbing the ladder to achieve your personal goals; it is about creating a legacy that extends beyond yourself. Success is about using the knowledge, experiences, and lessons you have gained to pave the way for others, ensuring the path becomes a little smoother for those who come after you. It is about recognizing that every step you take upward carries the potential to lift someone else.

When you experience your shift—when you break through barriers, overcome challenges, and step into your purpose, do not forget those who are still navigating the journey. Share your insights, be a mentor, and create opportunities for others to shine. Success is amplified when it is shared, and your willingness to guide and support others can create ripple effects that extend far beyond what you might imagine.

Helping others along the way is not just an act of kindness; it is a responsibility. You did not make it here alone. Somewhere along your journey, someone poured into you, believed in you, or opened a door for you. Paying it forward ensures that the cycle of growth and empowerment continues. Whether it is offering mentorship, sharing resources, or simply being a listening ear, your support can be the catalyst that helps someone else experience their own shift.

Remember, success is not measured by how high you climb but by how many people you inspire, uplift, and empower along the way. When you reach back to help others, you create a legacy of leadership, resilience, and collaboration—a legacy that lasts far longer than any single achievement.

Pay It Forward

- Identify one person in your circle you can mentor or support.

- Schedule a meeting or call to share your experiences and offer guidance.

Reflection Prompt: What's one piece of advice you wish someone had given you earlier in your career? Write it down and share it with someone who could benefit from it.

Lesson: Your journey isn't just about you; it's about creating a legacy of support and empowerment for those coming behind you, regardless of their background, identity, or experiences.

EXERCISE SIX:
STAYING MOTIVATED

"Keeping Your Cool When the Donuts Keep Coming in HOT"

Let's be honest—there will be days when the metaphorical donuts keep piling up, and you feel like shoving the entire box off the table. Seeing the same old hollow gestures instead of real opportunities can make you question your path. You might find yourself rolling your eyes, thinking, *"Seriously, we are still doing this?"*

But here is the truth: donuts will come and go, but your determination and focus are what will keep you moving forward. You cannot control how others lead, but you can control how you respond. This recipe is about staying motivated when it feels like the world is serving you donuts for breakfast, lunch, and dinner. Let us talk about how to lean into your faith, focus on your growth, and handle the "donuts" with grace and resilience.

When the glaze is blinding, and the frustration feels overwhelming, it is time to anchor yourself in your "why." Why are you here? Why did you start this journey? Your purpose is bigger than any donut moment—it is tied to your goals, your dreams, and the legacy you are building.

Take a few moments to write down your top three reasons for being in your current role or pursuing your career goals.

- Are you striving to build a better future for your family?

- Do you want to create opportunities for others?

- Is it about proving to yourself that you can thrive, no matter what obstacles are thrown your way?

- Keep this list in a place where you can see it daily—your desk, your planner, or even as a sticky note on your mirror. When the donuts threaten to derail you, revisit this list and let it remind you of the bigger picture.

Faith is what will carry you through the toughest times, especially when you feel unseen or undervalued. Trust that every challenge, even the ones that feel unfair, prepares you for something greater.

- Start each day with a moment of reflection or prayer, grounding yourself in your purpose.

- Find scriptures, affirmations, or quotes that uplift you and remind you of your strength. Keep them handy for when you need a quick reset during the day.

It is easy to get caught up in the donuts—why they are there, who is handing them out, and why nothing seems to change. But here is the thing: you cannot control the actions of others, only your own, so shift your focus.

- Instead of dwelling on what is missing, channel your energy into what you can create.

- Use donut moments as fuel to seek out opportunities for growth, whether that means learning a new skill, volunteering for a challenging project, or building relationships with those who value your contributions.

Reflection Prompt: Think about a time when you turned a frustrating situation into a stepping stone for success. What did you learn, and how did it help you grow? Write it down as a reminder of your ability to rise above. Yes, the donuts are frustrating, but do not let them rob you of the joy in your journey. Celebrate the small wins, find humor in the chaos, and remind yourself of how far you have come.

Celebrate Wins, Big and Small

- Did you go through a challenging meeting? Treat yourself to your favorite coffee.

- Received positive feedback from a colleague? Write it down and revisit it on tough days.

- Found a moment of calm amidst the chaos? Take a deep breath and pat yourself on the back for not snapping; you are doing a great job!

Lesson: Donuts may seem like obstacles, but they can be the very things that push you to grow. Each time you face a hollow gesture or unfulfilling moment, let it remind you of your strength, resilience, and purpose.

By focusing on your "why," leaning into your faith, and taking control of your narrative, you are not just surviving—you are thriving. And that, my friend, is how you turn a box of donuts into a feast for your success.

Now, take this mindset and move forward because real growth begins when you embrace the lessons in every donut moment.

EXERCISE SEVEN:
EMBRACE THE BIGGER PICTURE

"Do not get stuck on the donuts, take a step back and look at the bigger picture."

The donuts you see today won't define your entire journey. They're just a small part of a much larger picture. Think of them as speed bumps—not roadblocks. You're on a path that's leading somewhere greater, and each challenge is preparing you for the next level.

- Draw a timeline of your career. Mark the key moments where you've learned, grown, or overcome obstacles. Then, add where you want to go next.

- Visualize yourself at the "finish line" of this chapter. What does success look like? Write it down in vivid detail, as if it's already happened.

Reflection Prompt: What lesson can you learn from the donuts you're seeing right now? How might this moment be preparing you for the bigger picture?

Let's be honest, faith, in whatever form it takes for each of us, is what carries us through when everything else feels uncertain. There will be days when the donuts feel overwhelming, when you're questioning why you're even in the room. But remember, you are not just placed anywhere without a purpose. Your faith is your anchor, your guide, and your source of strength.

Create a Reflection Journal

- Dedicate a notebook or journal to your personal journey. Use it to write down prayers, meaningful quotes, scriptures, affirmations, or reflections that ground you and remind you of the promises that guide your life.

- Each week, take time to reflect on how your beliefs, values, or faith have helped you navigate challenges and stay motivated through difficult times.

Lesson: Sometimes the shift you are hoping for may feel delayed because there is work happening behind the scenes that you cannot see. Trust the process and the timing of something greater than yourself. The "donuts" of life—those temporary fixes—will fade, but the plan and purpose for your journey are lasting and meaningful.

EXERCISE EIGHT:
FIND MOTIVATION IN MENTORSHIP

"Share the recipe, and help others gather their ingredients for success."

When the donuts are testing your patience, and frustration feels like it's boiling over, it's time to redirect that energy into something meaningful, which is mentorship.

Helping others is not just about giving back; it's about reigniting your own sense of purpose and value.

Mentorship is like brewing a fresh pot of coffee on a tough morning—it re-energizes you, wakes up your potential, and reminds you why you're in the game.

By guiding someone else through their journey, you reflect on your own challenges and see the progress you've made. It's a win-win: you help someone else grow, and in the process, you grow too.

- *Identify Someone Who Could Benefit from Your Guidance.*

    o Look around your workplace or - community. Is there someone who is navigating the same challenges you once faced? Maybe it's a junior colleague struggling with their confidence or a peer unsure of their next step.

Take the first step and offer your support. Sometimes, all someone needs is for someone to say, "I see you, and I'm gonna help you."

- *Share Your Donut Moments*

  o Mentorship isn't just about celebrating wins; it's about being honest about the struggles too. Share a lesson you learned from dealing with those hollow gestures. Help them see how challenges, no matter how frustrating, can become opportunities for growth.

For example, tell them about the time you turned a donut moment like being passed over for a project into a chance to pitch your own idea. Showing vulnerability builds trust and reminds both you and your mentee of the strength that comes from resilience.

Reflection Prompt: What is one piece of advice you've given a mentee that also inspires you? Write it down and revisit it whenever you feel stuck or unmotivated. Sometimes, the advice you give to others is exactly what you need to hear for yourself.

Lesson: Mentorship is not just about teaching, it's about learning. It's about realizing that your experiences, both good and bad, have value. It's about taking the lessons from your donut moments and transforming them into tools for someone else's success.

When you pour into others, you create a ripple effect of growth, empowerment, and positivity. And here's the beautiful part: the more you help others rise, the more you'll feel yourself rising too.

So, the next time the donuts start piling up, remind yourself of this: you have the power to turn those empty gestures into something meaningful. By mentoring someone else, you're not just surviving, you're thriving and helping others thrive too.

EXERCISE NINE:
CHOOSE JOY DAILY

"Joy is the Glaze You Control."

Here's the truth—donuts do not have the power to steal your joy unless you hand it over. Each day presents you with a choice: to dwell on what is wrong or to celebrate what is right. This does not mean ignoring the challenges; it means refusing to let them define you. Choosing joy is about reclaiming your power and shifting your perspective.

Daily Gratitude Practice

- Start your day or wind it down by writing down three things you are grateful for. They can be monumental—like getting a glowing review—or simple, like the first sip of your favorite coffee or the smile from a coworker.

- Keep a "Joy Journal" nearby. Flip through it whenever the donuts start piling up to remind yourself of the good things that keep you grounded.

Celebrating the Small Wins

- Did you complete a tough task today? Celebrate.

- Did you set a boundary that protected your peace? Celebrate.

- Even if the win feels tiny, CELEBRATE. Joy thrives in recognition.

Reflection Prompt: What is something about your current role or life that brings you joy? How can you create more space for it daily? Write it down and revisit it as a source of strength when the donuts start appearing.

Lesson: Joy is not found; it is made. It is a deliberate choice to see the sweetness in your life, even when the glaze of challenges tries to blur your vision. Joy gives you clarity, resilience, and a reason to keep moving forward. Remember, while you cannot always control the donuts, you can control your reaction. Choose joy daily—it is the best recipe for thriving, no matter what life serves up.

EXERCISE TEN:
MOVING FORWARD

"Your journey is the ultimate dessert."

Donuts can slow you down, frustrate you, or even make you question your path, but here is the truth: they cannot stop you unless you let them. The key to thriving in the face of obstacles is simple—keep moving. Even the smallest steps will add up over time.

Think about it like walking up a hill; as long as you keep putting one foot in front of the other, you are still climbing.

Take Action, One Step at a Time

- Progress does not have to be dramatic or meaningful. Identify one actionable step you can take each week to move closer to your goals. It might be something small, like sending a LinkedIn message to a potential mentor, signing up for an online course to sharpen your skills, or updating your resume to reflect your most recent achievements.

Celebrate Your Wins

- Acknowledge every victory, no matter how small it seems. Did you finally speak up in a meeting? Celebrate it. Did you take time to reflect and map out your goals? Celebrate that too. Treat yourself to a coffee, a walk in the park, or simply a quiet moment to honor your efforts.

Track Your Growth

- Keep a journal or log of your weekly steps and wins. Over time, you will be amazed at how far you have come. This is not just about tracking progress, but about reminding yourself that you are capable and that every effort counts.

Motivational Mantra: "I am stronger than the donuts in my path. My purpose is bigger, my vision is clearer, and my faith is stronger."

Lesson: Moving forward is not about giant leaps; it is about consistent, intentional steps. The donuts may appear, but they are just distractions. Your purpose is the driving force that keeps you moving. So, whether you are walking, jogging, or sprinting toward your goals, know this: every bit of effort is a testament to your resilience, determination, and faith. Keep moving forward, because the best is yet to come.

CLOSING THOUGHTS:
DON'T LET THE DONUTS ROLL!

"I Got Donuts" is not just a book; it is a movement, a way of life, and a reminder that you are in control of your journey. This is about recognizing those hollow, sweet on-the-surface gestures for what they truly are, reclaiming your power, and charting a path that is uniquely yours. You are not here to settle; you are here to build something extraordinary, to leave your mark, and to create a legacy that cannot be erased.

Let us be honest, the donuts will always be there. They will show up as missed opportunities, unqualified leaders, and empty gestures dressed up as meaningful acts. But those donuts? They do not define you. What defines you is your ability to rise above, to keep moving, and to see the bigger picture. You are not someone who gets stuck in the glaze; you are someone who keeps pushing forward.

The journey you are on is not about waiting for someone to hand you what you deserve. It is about creating it for yourself. It is about knowing your worth, embracing your authenticity, and using every challenge as fuel for your growth. When the donuts show up, you will not flip the box or let frustration take over. Instead, you will pause, take a deep breath, and focus on the lessons, not the distractions.

Through everything, you must remember that your shift is coming. That breakthrough you have been working toward, praying for, and visualizing—is on the way. And when it arrives, you will be ready, not just because you did the work, but because you believed in yourself every step of the way. You stayed grounded in your purpose, rooted in your faith, and committed to your goals. That is what makes the difference.

So here is the promise: the next time a metaphorical donut comes your way—whether it is a hollow compliment, a missed opportunity, or someone doubting your potential—you will keep your cool. You will see it for what it is and keep moving forward. You have bigger things to do, and donuts, while tempting, are just distractions. You are not here to settle for crumbs; you are here to take the whole bakery.

This book is filled with lessons, humor, and hard truths, but above all, it is a reminder of your power. You are not defined by the obstacles you face but by how you rise above them. You are a leader, a trailblazer, and an inspiration. Your story is yours to write, and it is beautiful, twists and turns included.

The world needs your shine, your leadership, and your light. So, step into your shift with grace, humor, and determination. Build your legacy, embrace your lessons, and leave the donuts in the breakroom. You are unstoppable, and the world is waiting to see what you will do next. Shine bright, because you are the real treat.

We Got This, Y'all!

ABOUT THE AUTHOR

Marquetta Toshe' Hemphill is a bold story-teller, speaker, and leadership voice with a heart for people and a spirit deeply rooted in faith. A proud Mississippi native, Marquetta brings a wealth of experience from years spent navigating dynamic workplace environments, where she developed a passion for cultivating authentic leadership, fostering inclusive growth, and creating spaces that empower others to thrive.

With a background that spans operations, marketing, leadership, and mentorship, Marquetta brings a well-rounded and relatable perspective shaped by real-life experiences. She understands that even in well-intentioned environments, individuals can still feel overlooked or unsure of how to grow. Rather than retreat in those moments, Marquetta chose to rise to use her voice, embrace her authenticity, and create space for others to do the same.

She is the founder of *I Got Donuts!* Enterprises, a platform dedicated to empowering professionals to reclaim their voice, own their story, and challenge outdated norms with confidence. Whether she's mentoring rising talent, speaking on stages, or sharing her personal testimony, Marquetta's message is consistent and clear: you don't have to shrink to succeed.

When she's not writing or leading change, she's raising two amazing daughters, vibing with her husband, styling power looks or sipping on a good cup of coffee while dreaming up her next big move.

I Got Donuts! is her debut book, a courageous, heartfelt, yet empowering journey that reminds readers: your story matters, your voice is powerful, and your light was never meant to be dimmed.

Interested in Publishing a Book?
Visit A2ZBooksPublishing.net